Looking Seaward Again

by

Sir Walter Runciman

Looking Seaward Again
by Sir Walter Runciman

ISBN: 978-93-63053-28-1

Published by

DOUBLE 9 BOOKS

2/13-B, Ansari Road
Daryaganj, New Delhi – 110002
info@double9books.com
www.double9books.com
Tel. 011-40042856

CONTENTS

PREFACE

The following tales have been told to some few men and women by the fireside. The stories themselves only claim to be unvarnished matters of fact; and I may repeat here what I said in a previous volume, that my object has not been to strain after literary effect or style. My too early desertion of home-life to graduate in the harsh and whimsical discipline of sailing-vessels in the days when they had still some years to live and "carry on" ere steam took the wind out of their sails, precluded such studies as are natural to the embryo man of letters. But the circumstances that told against mere study did not prevent my preserving many memories of my sojourns ashore and voyages in distant seas. I mention this fact, not as an apology, but as an explanation which I hope may commend itself to the amiable reader.

WALTER RUNCIMAN.

3rd December 1907.

Through Torpedoes and Ice

"Osman the Victorious," as Skobeleff called the matchless Turkish pasha, had kept the Russian hordes at bay for one hundred and forty-two days. Never in the annals of warfare had the world beheld such unexpected military genius, combined with stubborn endurance, as was shown during the siege of Plevna. On December 10th, 1877, Osman came out and made a desperate struggle to break through the Russian lines; but after four hours' hard fighting the Turks sent up the white flag, and boisterous cheering swelled over the snow-clad land when it became known that the greatest Turkish general of modern times had surrendered. His little army of Bashi-Bazouks had annihilated more than one Siberian battalion. The Russian loss was forty thousand, and the Turkish thirty thousand. Had Suleiman and the other Turkish generals shown the same stubborn spirit as Osman, the Russian army would never have been permitted to cross the Balkans, much less reach Constantinople.[1] But after the fall of Plevna the resistance of the Turkish army was feeble, and the Muscovites were not long in pitching their camp at San Stefano. Indeed, a rumour got abroad one night that the Russians were in the suburbs of Constantinople. This roused the indignation of the English jingoes to such a pitch that the great Jewish Premier, with the dash that characterized his career, gave peremptory orders for the British fleet to proceed, with or without leave, through the Dardanelles, and if any resistance was shown to silence the forts. Russia protested and threatened, and Turkey winked a stern objection, but Lord Beaconsfield was firm, and suitable arrangements were arrived at between the Powers.

Bismarck offered his services as mediator, and suggested that a European Congress should be held at Berlin to discuss the contents of the Treaty of San Stefano. This was agreed to, and Lord Beaconsfield, accompanied by Lord Salisbury, were the British representatives at the Congress. The Prime Minister and the Foreign Secretary drove a hard and favourable bargain for Turkey and for Britain. Turkey, it is needless to say, got the worst of it; but, considering her crushing defeat, came well out of the settlement. Cyprus was ceded to the British, to be used as a naval station, and subsequent experience has proved the wisdom of this acquisition. Lord Beaconsfield proclaimed to a tumultuous crowd on the occasion of his return to London that he had brought back "peace with honour." This was the acme of the great Jew's fame. It looked as though he could have done anything he liked with the British people, so that it is no wonder that the old man lost his balance when such homage was paid him by that section of the public which was smitten with his picturesque and audacious personality.

Naturally, his policy impregnated Russia with a strong anti-British feeling, and it was said that her activity in running up earthworks and apparently impregnable fortifications was in anticipation of Disraeli declaring war and ordering the fleet to bombard the Crimean ports; hence, too, in addition to the strong fortifications, torpedo mines were laid for miles along the seaboard, and every possible means and opportunity were taken to make it widely known that the Black Sea was one deadly mine-field. The Press on all sides was, as usual, brimful of reports of the most alarmist nature—these, of course, for the most part extravagant and inaccurate rumours. Nor did the Russian Press minimize accounts of the terrible devastation that was wrought on unarmed trespassers who came within the zone of terror. I read twice of my own rapid and complete destruction. There is no doubt that mines were laid, though both their capacity for destruction and the number of them was very much exaggerated.

From the end of —— outer breakwater to beyond the —— there was a line of mines which left between the land and them a channel less than half a mile wide. A gunboat with torpedo pilots aboard was moored at the south end, and vessels prior to the war and during the armistice were compelled to take a pilot in and out; but no vessel was allowed to pass in or out from sunset to sunrise. A gunboat was also stationed outside the inner breakwater. A large fleet of steamers had been attracted by the high freights, inflated by the war fever that permeated Europe at that time, and also because the season was far advanced, and merchants were anxious to get their stuff shipped in case hostilities broke out. The heavy snowstorms had made the roads almost impassable, but in spite of great difficulties the loading was carried on; slowly, it is true, but with dogged perseverance. The frost had become keen, and large floes of ice were rushed down the reaches by the swift current. Booms were moored outside the vessels to protect them, but these were constantly being carried away, and not a little damage was done. A consultation amongst the captains was held as to the advisability of leaving with what cargoes they had aboard, but only two decided to start on the following morning. Some of the others said they could force their way through six inches of ice, and would risk waiting to receive their whole cargo. Accordingly, as soon as it was daylight one of the captains who had made all arrangements to leave gave orders to unmoor. The other had changed his mind, and fell in with the views of the majority. The captain of the *Claverhouse*, however, got underweigh, but before getting very far his engineer reported that the hot-well cover had broken in two. It was temporarily repaired, and she got along famously until they came to a bend in the river where there was much packed ice. For two hours manoeuvring continued without any appreciable result. At last the big mass began to move, and a navigable channel was opened, which enabled the vessel to make slow though risky progress through a field of moving ice.

The anchorage at — — was reached before darkness set in, and a vessel which had left four days previously was observed to be ashore, with the ice drifting up against her port side, forcing her farther on to the bank. Signals were hoisted offering assistance, but before the reply could be made a blinding snowstorm came on, which lasted all through the night. The next morning, at daylight, signals were again made by the *Claverhouse* to the stranded vessel asking if they would accept assistance. The reply came, "I want lighters." The crew were jettisoning the cargo of wheat on to the ice as it flowed past, but the more they lightened the farther the vessel was forced on to the bank by the rushing current. The master of the *Claverhouse*, observing the critical position, sent a boat away with a small line. A communication was effected, but not without great difficulty. The master of the *Aureola* was worn out with anxiety and want of rest, for his vessel had been ashore for forty-eight hours. He very wisely accepted the assistance which had opportunely come to him. A tow-rope was attached to the small line, and by this means a thick tow-line was got aboard, and she was dragged off the bank; then orders were unaccountably given to cut the tow-rope. This very nearly resulted in a more serious disaster, as the engineers in the confusion kept the engines going astern, and the rope drifting with the current, became entangled round the propeller. If the anchor and chains had not held the great strain that was put on them, she would have gone ashore again in a worse position, and inevitably have broken her back. As it was, the propeller was cleared in about a couple of hours. The captain of the *Aureola* was not well acquainted with the locality, and arranged that he should follow the other steamer to— —. Suitable plans and signals were settled, and both vessels weighed anchor and proceeded as fast through the ice as was compatible with safety. Once out of the narrows and clear of the obstruction, the engines were put at full speed and kept going until they were forced to slow down on account of the snow squalls, which obscured everything. The sea had become rough, and the utmost resources of the commanders were taxed in their efforts to navigate the coast and yet keep together. They groped their way until — — town lights were visible. It was then seen that the gunboat anchored at the south end of the mine-field was signalling to them to stop; but still they went slowly on, feeling their way by the lead, while those aboard the gunboat began to fire rockets with exciting rapidity. Regardless of the warning, the two steamers kept on their way until they got to the anchorage, when the warship was hidden from view.

It was past midnight; and although the crews of both vessels had gone through a severe ordeal of physical endurance, they were each anxious to hear what the other had to say about the events of the last forty-eight hours, which were beset with peril, and had culminated by boldly running into the anchorage over the mines in defiance of the regulations—to say nothing of the danger of being blown up, or the mysterious prospect of Siberia! The captain of the *Aureola* was greatly perturbed, and he promptly ordered his gig to be manned to take him to the *Claverhouse*. On getting aboard, he reproached his friend for leading him into what might prove a serious scrape. The two men talked long of the exciting doings of the day and the policy that should be adopted on the morrow, when they would be confronted with officials that were not over well-disposed to British subjects. They fully realized that the case would have to be managed with great astuteness, so they bethought themselves of one of the cleverest and most popular men in——, and sent a message to him asking his help. His name need not be mentioned; he is long since dead, and it is sufficient to say that he was an educated Maltese, and held a kind of magnetic influence over the harbour authorities. The Admiral was an amiable man in an ordinary way, and susceptible to the temptations that beset officials in these places; but the *Claverhouse's* offence was no common one, nor could it be approached in an ordinary way of speech.

On going ashore, the captains were ushered into the presence of the infuriated official who was to decide their destiny. He fumed and foamed savagely, and whenever an attempt was made to speak his paroxysms became inhuman. Their Maltese friend had come to their aid, and was waiting patiently for the storm to subside, so that he could explain how it happened that the regulations came to be broken. Things looked black until Mr. C—— began to speak in Russian. It took him some time to get the great man pacified, and as soon as that was accomplished he said to the master of the *Claverhouse*—"You know that you could be sent to Siberia or less. How am I to explain it? Why did you not keep at sea all night? There is only one thing that will save you."

"Well, then," responded the captain of the *Claverhouse*, "let that one thing be arranged; but let me also state the cause of our breaking the law. We could have kept the sea quite well had we known exactly where we were, but we could see nothing, and had to navigate by taking soundings, and as soon as we got into seven fathoms the water became smooth, and, fearing we might run aground, the anchor was let go. As for the rockets that were fired by the gunboat, we had passed the line of torpedoes before our attention was attracted by the firing. The Admiral himself could not have avoided it. Surely he cannot think we deliberately ran into the anchorage?"

"That is just what he does think," said Mr. C——. "What am I to do?"

"Settle on the best terms," said the captain.

At this point two officers took the captains to another room, and they were locked in. An hour afterwards Mr. C—— came to them and said—

"I have managed to get him quietened down. You have had a narrow squeak. It took me a long time to get him to speak of liberating you, and now I am requested to bring you to him so that you may be severely reprimanded. He talked of gaol, and sending you out of the country for ever, and inflicting a heavy fine; but that stage has passed, so come with me."

When they were ushered into the Admiral's presence he frowned severely at them. Russian officers and high officials always expect you to tremble when they administer a rebuke. Needless to say, the reception was harsh. There was a good deal of long stride, prancing from one end of the room to the other, vehement talk in Russian, and wild gesticulation. The Maltese told the somewhat callous captains that the Admiral declared the next Englishman that attempted such a thing, if he were not blown up, would have to be shot. An example must be made. The genial intermediary interjected with apparent sternness—

"Captains, you must apologize for the crime you have committed, and be thankful that you are going to be dealt leniently with. The Admiral is right: you deserved to be blown up with your ship. But apologize suitably, and leave the rest to me."

All but the last sentence was interpreted to the gallant official. An apology was made, and silently accepted; but the real penalty was not disclosed to the captains until afterwards, and then it was kept secret by them and by the two contracting parties. The two commanders, when being congratulated on their release, said they did not know what all the fuss was about. They had done no harm to anybody, and if hostilities were resumed they hoped the Turks would wipe the Russians off the field, and so on.

Three stirring months passed before the *Claverhouse* returned to ----. When she arrived at the gunboat guarding the torpedo channel, she took a pilot, and proceeded into the harbour in a law-abiding manner, while her captain, audibly and inaudibly, declaimed against a Government whose barbarous notions led them to impose restrictions that caused expense and interrupted the normal process of navigation. "What right have these beastly Russians to hamper British shipping like this?"

When the captain landed he was met by several friends, who cheerfully inquired if he had found another new channel into the port. He jokingly retorted—

"No; but I might have to find a new one out."

He was solemnly advised not to attempt it. The Admiral, whom he occasionally met, was unusually cordial, and this attitude of courtesy was ungrudgingly reciprocated. One evening the captain wished to visit a friend of his, whose vessel lay at the forts. The sentry asked him to retire. He refused to move, and commenced to harangue the soldier in a language he supposed to be Russian. There must have been something wrong about it, for after a few words of conversation the sentry rushed at him with the bayonet fixed, and but for the swiftness of his heels there might have been a tragedy. He immediately called at the Admiral's office, informed him of what had occurred, and requested that he should be escorted where he desired to go. An officer was sent with him, and when they got to the sentry the officer spoke to the man in a heated tone, and then slapped him on the face with the flat of his hand. The captain asked why he had struck the sentry. The officer replied—

"Because he told me you had used some Russian language to him that caused him to believe you were a suspicious character. I told him he was a fool, and that you were a friend of mine and of the Admiral. You will have no more trouble."

A *douceur* was slipped into the willing hand, and on the return journey another was given to the poor sentry, who showed a meekness and gratitude that was nearly pathetic.

On the following day there was a sensational rumour that the armistice would be raised and hostilities between the two belligerents resumed. At the forts and at the military quarters of the city there was much activity. The troops were being reviewed by one of the Grand Dukes, and there were evidences of conscription everywhere. Aboard the warships the flutter was quite noticeable, and the frequent communications between them and the shore augured trouble. Merchants, agents, and captains displayed unusual energy to complete their engagements. A strongly-worded order was handed to the captains of the few vessels still remaining in port that, on penalty of being sunk by the warships or blown up by torpedoes, no vessel was to go out of the port after sundown at 6 p.m.

On the second day after this instruction was given the loading of the *Claverhouse's* cargo was completed. A gentleman sent a note requesting the captain to see him, and not to remove the staging between his vessel and the quay, as it would be required to carry out an important shipment which would be of great benefit to himself and all concerned. Negotiations were opened, and were briefly as follows: — This estimable Briton had been approached by a person of great astuteness and easy integrity, who was neither an Englishman nor a Turk, to engage at all costs a steamer to take bullocks on deck to a certain unnamed destination. The freight would be paid before the cattle were shipped, but the vessel would have to sail that night, and a large sum would be paid for running that risk.

"State your price," said the genial agent; "anything within reason will be paid."

The captain was as eager to do a deal as his new acquaintance, though he pleaded the almost impossible task of running out of the port without being observed, and if observed the inevitable consequence of being sunk, probably with all on board. The agent, having in mind his own considerable interest, played discreetly on the vanity of the commander, and laughed at the notion of an astute person like him allowing himself to be trapped; appealed to his nationality, and the glory of having run out of a port that was severely blockaded. The captain cut this flow of greasy oratory short by stating that for the moment he was thinking of the amount of hard cash he was going to get, and not of the glory.

"I know what I will have to do, and I think I know how it will have to be done; but first let us fix the amount I am to have for doing it. My price is £——. Do you agree?"

"Yes," said the agent; "though it's a bit stiff. But the animals must go forward."

The captain did not expect so sudden a confirmation, and remarked, "I fancy I have not put sufficient value on the services I am to carry out; but I have given my word, and will keep it."

In due course the money was handed over in British gold. The cattle were taken aboard, and just as the sun was setting the moorings were cast off, and the vessel proceeded to the outer harbour and anchored. The chief mate was instructed to put as little chain as possible out, and the engineer was told to have a good head of steam at a certain hour. Meanwhile, the captain proceeded to the city to clear his ship, and at the stated hour he was stealthily rowed alongside. The pawls of the windlass were muffled, and the anchor was hove noiselessly up by hand; the engines were set easy ahead, and as soon as she was on her course the telegraph rang "full speed." She had not proceeded far before a shot was fired from the inner gunboat, which landed alongside the starboard quarter. The chief officer called from the forecastle head—

"They are firing at us—hadn't you better stop?"

"Stop, be d— —d! Do you want to be hung or sent to the Siberian mines?"

The next shot fell short of the stern. They now came thick and heavy, but the *Claverhouse* by this time was racing away, and was quickly out of range. The most critical time arrived when she was rushed headlong over the line of torpedoes; and as soon as the outer gunboat was opened clear of the breakwater, she, too, commenced to fire. Once the line of mines was safely passed, the course was set to hug the land. The firing from the torpedo gunboat was wildly inaccurate, never a shot coming within fathoms of their target, and soon the little steamer was far beyond the reach of the Tsar's guns.

Her captain had no faith in the report industriously circulated that the Crimean coast and the Black Sea were impenetrably mined, so he proceeded gaily on his voyage, shaking hands with himself for having succeeded in running the gauntlet without a single man being hurt, or the breaking of a rope-yarn. The crew were boisterously proud of the night's exploit. They knew that no pecuniary benefit would be derived by them, and were content to believe that they had been parties to a dashing piece of devil-may-care work. The average British sailor of that period loved to be in a scrape, and revelled in the sport of doing any daring act to get out of it. It never occurred to the captain that his crew might jib at the thought of undertaking so perilous a course. He had been reared in the courage of the class to which he belonged, and his confidence in the loyalty of his men was not shaken by the thoughtless interjection of the chief officer, who, in a shameful moment asked him to turn back after the first shot was fired. He had no time to think of that senseless advice when it was given, but it may be taken for granted the cautious mate did not add to his popularity with the crew. He had commanded large sailing vessels in the Australian passenger trade, and this was his first voyage in steam. The new life, with all its varied sensationalisms, was a mystery to him, and this little incident did not increase his belief in the wisdom of his change from sail to steam. He explained that the thought of what he regarded as inevitable disaster caused him to spontaneously call out that they were firing.

"Besides," he continued, "I don't like the business; so I'll resign my position and go back to sailing vessels again, on the completion of the voyage."

The captain reminded him of the fine spirit of enterprise that prevailed amongst the crew; only in a lesser degree, perhaps, than that which caused Nelson under different circumstances to say of his sailors, "They really mind shot no more than peas."

"Nelson may have said that, and our crew may have a fine spirit of wholesale daring, but I don't like to be mixed up with either the enterprise or the shot," retorted the reflective officer; and I daresay if the captain were asked for an opinion now he would be disposed to take the mate's view.

The thought of being pursued kept up a quiet excitement. The vessel was pressed through the water at her maximum speed and arrived at her first destination without any mishap to herself or the deck cargo, which was landed expeditiously. She then continued on her voyage. On arrival at the discharging port, a letter was received from the owners complimenting the captain on the success of an undertaking which would contribute so considerably to the profits of the voyage, and at the same time calling his attention to a newspaper cutting. An official telegram to the English Press stated that *"A British steamer, name unknown, in attempting to run out of — — harbour over the torpedo lines, was warned and fired upon by a Russian warship which was guarding the harbour. The steamer refused to stop. She was shelled, and in crossing the mine zone the vessel, with her crew, was blown to atoms!"* This was a sensational piece of news to read of one's self.

Two years elapsed before the captain again steamed into — — harbour. He expected to meet his old friend the Admiral, and a few other Russian gentlemen in whom his interest was centred; but they had either gone to their rest or had been removed. It seemed as though the incident that caused so much commotion at the time had passed out of recollection. Indeed, there seemed quite a new order of things. New officials were there. The gunboats were removed from their familiar stations. The torpedoes that had been the dread of navigators had been lifted, and it was commonly reported that many of them were loaded with sand. No signs were visible of there having been war defences that were meant to be regarded as impregnable—and it is not to be denied the earthworks justified that opinion. There were whisperings that when those in high places discovered what some of the mines were charged with, the persons responsible for the laying of the mines were seized; and tradition has it that an impromptu scaffold had been erected outside the town, and every one of the suspects hanged without trial—and merely on the suspicion that they knew of, even if they had not contributed to, the treacherous act. In the light of the horrors that are occurring in Russia at the present time, it is not improbable that there was treachery; and that when it was discovered, suspicion centred on certain persons, who were, in accordance with Muscovite autocracy, dispatched without ceremony, guilty or not guilty.

"Ah!" said Mr. C— — to the captain, who had just finished describing his last departure from — — Harbour, "you may thank your stars that the torpedoes were loaded with sand or some other rubbish, or you wouldn't have been here this day. The officers were in a great fury at the wires not operating when you were running out, and the men—submarines, I think, they are called—who were behind the earthworks were knocked about badly. They came to my place to get to know the name of the vessel, but I bamboozled them, and gave them cigars and vodka, and they weren't long in forgetting about what had happened. I think there is no doubt about your being the cause of having the mines raised, as, to my certain knowledge, they tried to explode them the day after you left the port, and very few of them went off. Things were kept a bit quiet, but I can always get to know what is going on, and if the gunboats had been properly handled that night it would have been all up with you."

"But," said the captain, "what on earth is the use of talking that way! They were not properly handled, and here I am. And what I want to know is this: do you think there will be any more about it, now the war is over, and old Pumper Nichol [the Admiral] and his friends are not here?"

"I don't know," said his friend. "You never can tell what these sly rascals are thinking or doing; but I will know as soon as there are any indications. If I had been you, I wouldn't have come out here so soon; or, at least, have first made sure that all danger was over. But never mind; we'll soon smuggle you off, if we can get the slightest hint. 'Palm oil squares the yards,' as the old sailors used to say, and nobody has had more experience of that than I."

"Does G——d and old J——b know about the affair?"

"I think they are bound to, though they may have forgotten. Anyhow, they are absolutely loyal, and may be depended upon if their aid is called into requisition. Do you know they had to clear out of the country with their families, and nearly every English family had to do the same?"

"Well, Patrovish C——," said the captain, "they may seize the steamer, but they will never be allowed to seize me, even should it be legal to do so, now the war is at an end."

"What do they care about what is legal," said Patrovish. "If it suits their purpose, and those in authority learn what took place, there will be no scruples about doing anything. My advice is to keep quiet and cool-headed, and I feel almost certain you won't be interfered with. But there comes Yaunie. Hear what he says."

This gentleman was a Greek pilot, who had previously been a boatswain aboard a Greek sailing-vessel. He saw an excellent opening at the beginning of the steamship era to add to his income, so commenced a business which flourished so well that his riches were the envy of a large residential public, to say nothing of the seafaring itinerants who swarmed in and out of the port. He spoke English with a Levantine accent. Physically, he was a fine-looking, well-built man, who commanded attention and respect from everybody. He was on excellent terms with the port authorities, and with sea captains, and deemed it part of a well thought-out policy to share with popular shrewdness a portion of his takings. His benevolence was more partially shown towards the officials than to those from whom he derived his income; but because of his geniality, and—mostly, I should say—on account of his generosity, he was well liked by both sections of people. He was quite uneducated, and, like most clever men who have this misfortune, he had great natural gifts. His memory was prodigious, and he invested his savings with the judgment of an expert, keeping mental accounts with startling accuracy; but, notwithstanding this, his memory never retained anything he conceived it to be policy to forget. When asked his opinion as to whether there was any likelihood of anything more being heard of the captain's running out of the harbour and over the torpedoes, he suggestively put his finger to his mouth, and said—

"I can know nothing, but I tink it is over." And shrugging his broad shoulders, he 'cutely remarked, "Some dead, some maybe Siberia, and"—with a significant smile he lowered his voice to a whisper—"some, maybe, 'fraid to say anything because for many reason. Yes, I tink finis; but if not, den you trust me to help. I knows these people, and some of dem knows me."

Yaunie was taken fully into the confidence of the captain and Patrovish, and when he took his leave they felt sure that to have him as a friend was of great value in the event of the affair being resurrected. The captain had renewed many old friendships, and spent his evenings in the hospitable homes of an English colony whose kindness is unequalled anywhere. Unlike most English families who settle in foreign countries, they retained a great many of their national customs in food, and also in their mode of life generally. Of course the extremes of climate have to be considered, but all their homes preserve their British atmosphere.

The *Claverhouse* had nearly completed loading, and the kindly emissaries of her captain had reported nothing of a disturbing character, until one morning a steamer came in and was moored alongside the *Claverhouse*. Yaunie was the pilot, and after completing his work he went aboard the *Claverhouse* and asked to see the captain.

"He is not astir yet," said the steward.

"I must speak with him at once," said Yaunie.

The captain, overhearing the conversation, called out, "All right, come to my room."

"Well, Yaunie, what news this morning?" asked the captain.

"Ah, it is very bad news," replied Yaunie. "That fool Farquarson," pointing to where the other steamer lay, "speaks all the time about what happened when you went from the port without permission. He say that he was aboard the gunboat asking for a torpedo channel-pilot, and that he could not get one because they were firing at you all the time. They asked him the name of the steamer, but he told some other. I say to him he was wrong, but he say no; and he will jabb, as you call it."

"Well, Yaunie, what's to be done? What is the remedy?"

"What's to be done—I don' know what you call the other. I say, get the steamer loaded quick and away. I don' tink trouble, but O Chresto! his tong go like steam-winch, and you much better Black Sea dan here."

"Very excellent advice, Yaunie. Now let us go on deck."

A sudden inspiration came to the captain, which caused him to exclaim—

"Yaunie, I'll ask him to eat with us. This is our English mode of settling obstacles, and making and retaining friendships. Don't you think it a good suggestion?"

"Do anything you like. Give him the Sacrament, but keep him quiet. He is very dangerous now."

The captain of the other steamer was on deck, and as soon as he got his eye on them he bellowed out in terms of unjustifiable familiarity—

"Hallo, old fellow, how are ye? So they've not sent ye to the silver mines yet?"

"No," smartly retorted the captain, with some warmth, "they've not, or I wouldn't have been here. But they d—d soon will if you don't keep your mouth shut!"

Without heeding what was said to him, the distinguished commander of the new-comer slapped his thigh vigorously with his right hand, and laughed out—

"By Joshua, you were in a tight corner, and will never be nearer being popped! [sunk]. They were furious at me, and would have blown all England up because I said I didn't know who it was."

"Oh," said the *Claverhouse's* commander, "that is old history. Come aboard and have breakfast with me."

"All right," said Farquarson, "I'll have a wash up, and then come. But what a darned funny thing not to blow you up with the mines. I just said to my mate, they are a lot of lazy beasts, or there's something wrong with the wires. But the mate said, 'No; he's taken them unawares.' 'Unawares be d——d!' said I; 'he's not taken these gunboat chaps unawares, for I couldn't get them to stop firing.'"

"He's off again!" interjected Yaunie.

"All right, all right!" replied the impatient captain to his voluble compatriot. "Come to breakfast as quick as you can, there's a good fellow."

Farquarson got to the companion-way—*i.e.* the entrance to the cabin—and was about to make some further remarks when the captain of the *Claverhouse* said to Yaunie, "Let's go below, for God's sake! As long as he sees us he'll keep on."

When they got into the cabin, the burly pilot was almost inarticulate. All he could say was—

"My goodness, what a tong! He must be dangerous to his owners. I have never see such a tong."

In due course the irrepressible person appeared, and was received with professional cordiality. He had no sooner taken his seat at the table than he became convulsed with laughter, slapped his hand on the table, and shouted—

"By Cocker, I'll never forget it! The rage of them Russians, and the way they blazed away their shot, and it never going within miles of where you were! Miles, mind you!"

Yaunie and his friend looked at each other in savage despair, as he persisted in reeling off quantities of disconnected incoherencies. But relief to his perturbed friends came when the steward placed the breakfast on the table. He stopped the flow of narration, and exclaimed—

"Ah! that's what I like—dry hash and a bit of ham with an egg or two. I was just saying to my mate—who's as big a born fool as ever drank whisky—there's not a better meal made at sea than dry hash."

By this time his mouth was full, and it was difficult to know what he wished to convey. His eating was quite as boundless as his talk, though he could not do both at once. Having finished a good sound plate of hash, he passed his plate along for some ham and eggs, and asked his host if he did not observe what a good appetite he had compared with what he used to have.

"Yes," said the captain, in blissful ignorance of what he was saying. "Your appetite was never very good. I'm glad to see you making such a good breakfast."

"Well, you know," replied the guest, "the worst of me is, I appear to be unsociable when I'm eating, as I cannot both eat and talk."

"Go on eating, then," said the host.

"Yes, go on eatin'," responded Yaunie. "You had a long passage, and must be hungry."

"Quite right," replied the guest, with his mouth full. "I'm glad you don't think me uncivil, but as I say, I like my breakfast better than most meals, and I can only do one thing at a time. My wife always says I must have been born either eating or talking."

He laughed heartily at this little domestic joke, and proceeded with the putting in of the "bunker coals," as he called it. The captain of the *Claverhouse* and the pilot had purposely lingered over their meal to keep him company. He observed this, and effusively asked them not to mind him a bit, and to leave the table if they wanted to. After expressing a few unreal excuses for their apparent rudeness, they were prevailed upon to go into the state-room, where the captain solemnly conveyed to Yaunie that he never thought he would live to have imposed upon him such humiliation.

"I hope the brute will have an apoplectic fit!" said he.

Yaunie did not quite understand all that was said, but knew it meant some form of obliquy, and replied, "Yes, and I hope so too."

As soon as Farquarson had finished eating, he straightway came to the state-room and assured his host that he never remembered enjoying a breakfast so much.

"Let's have a cigar," said he, "to soothe my nerves a bit."

This was given him. He lit up, and was proceeding to discuss the merits of good feeding with great volubility when his harangue was snapped by a request from his host to "cut it," as he wished to have a yarn with him about a matter which was of great importance to himself. "In short, I wish you to be most careful not to attract attention to me by any friendly comment about that affair of two years ago. No one who is in office now would appear to have any suspicion of what took place; or if they do, it is obvious they are not desirous of opening the question up again. But should it be brought prominently before them, they will have to do something, and it may make it very awkward for me. Now, what I want you to do for me is this: never mention the incident again. I am sure you would not intentionally do anything that would jeopardize my safety, and I feel that I have only to ask and you will give me your word not to do it."

Farquarson jumped to his feet, gripped the hand of the captain in a sailorly fashion, and said—

"On my Masonic honour, I swear never to breathe again what you have warned me against, and I'm glad you told me. I might innocently have got you into a nasty mess. It never struck me when I was bawling out to you that there was danger. But between ourselves, it was a bit thick your dashing out of the 'impregnable port,' as they called it, and expectin' to get off scot-free, I have often spun long twisters about it, and you can bet it was always made attractive."

"I feel sure you would do that, Farquarson, as you were always a good story-teller."

This encouraging flattery switched his mind with eager interest on to a subject quite irrelevant to the one which had engaged their attention so long.

"Yes," said he, with a self-satisfied smile, "that's true. But talking about yarns, you remember when I was with Milburn's, running to Hamburg? The old gentleman asked me to take a few overmen a trip. They belonged to some mine he was interested in. By the time we got outside, and got the decks cleared up, it was dark, and the watch was set. The look-out man went on to the topgallant forecastle, and I was walking from side to side of the bridge when one of the miners came running up, and in great excitement he said—

"'Captain, for God's sake gan doon to the cabin and pacify them! They're playin' nap, and they've faalen oot amang theirselves, and there's fair almighty hell gannin' on. Aa's sure if ye divvent get them pacified ther'll be morder!'

"'My good man,' I said, 'I cannot leave the bridge.'

"'Ye canna' leave the bridge! What for, then?'

"'Because,' I said, 'I must keep a look-out and see that that man on the forecastle-head does the same. If he were to see me leave the bridge, the chances are he would get careless and sit down and go to sleep, and we might run into something, and probably sink ourselves or somebody else and lose a lot of lives.'

"By this time I heard loud voices and awful oaths coming from the after-end of the ship, so says I, 'This must be put a stop to, but I cannot leave here without somebody takin' my place. You must take it, and walk across and across as I am doing, so that that fellow on the look-out will think it's me.'

"'Aa'm not pertikler what aa dee, mister, if ye ony get thor differences settled before ye come up. Aa nivor heerd sic swearin'.'

"'Very well,' said I; 'you do what I've told you to do. Walk steadily to and fro, and I'll go and see what can be done.'

"When I got down below they were still wrangling, but I soon made peace with them, and they asked me to have a hand with them. I had a look on deck. It was a fine moonlight night, and nothing seemed to be in the way, so I began to play, and forgot all about the fellow on the bridge, and everything else for that matter, until I heard four bells go. This reminded me, so I stopped short, went on to the poop, and the other fellows came up with me. I was chaffing them about their row, and I heard the look-out man call out, 'A red light on the port bow, sir!' I saw we were going a long way clear, so took no notice; but the miner on the bridge increased his pace. In less than a minute the look-out man called out again, 'A red light on the port bow,' and got no answer. I thought to myself, 'What's going to be the upshot of this?' when the man called out again, sharply this time, 'A red light on the port bow!' The miner quite excitedly shouted at the top of his voice, 'Blaw the b— —y thing oot, then, and let's hear ne mair aboot it!'"

At this conclusion the two captains laughed heartily, and so did Yaunie. Then all at once Farquarson began as suddenly as he had left off—

"Now, let us make up our minds never to broach running the gauntlet again in Russian waters, for they're devils to listen, and you never know where they are. Why, I've seen them at the time of the war crawlin' and sneakin' about all over, lying on the sofa in the billiard-rooms, and come and ask you to play in good English. Sometimes the impudent villains would come and barefacedly sit down at the same table where you were having a meal, and begin speakin' and get you to say something disrespectful about Russia and their Tzar, and lots of poor fellows were asked to leave the country for it. Talk about despotism and bribery! Well, I've seen some of their goings on. What did they do when the poor Turks that were taken prisoners when Plevna fell marched into Reval? A few of us cheered them, and the Russians got quite annoyed about it, and hustled us about as though we were common thieves, and threatened to run us into their filthy gaol. My word, how things have altered since the days when you could kill a Russian and nobody cared a brass button! But now—well, there's no word to express it."

"Ah! they're a cruel, merciless lot," interjected Captain S—; "but I think you are getting excited, Farquarson, so you better cease talking about them."

"It is time I was getting up to the city. They are rattling it into her. She'll be loaded in a jiffy, and I've much to do."

"Very well," said the bluff skipper, "get away. And it's understood that mum's the word; but mind you're not through the wood yet. What do you say, Yaunie?"

"I say you no speak so loud or so much. It is better not."

"Very well, old skin-the-goat," said Farquarson playfully; "I suppose I am a bit noisy."

He then jumped aboard his vessel, and invited the trusty pilot to follow him so that they might work out a scheme that would thwart any possibility of a raid being made on the *Claverhouse*. He prided himself on being fertile in strategy, and certainly his notions were not those of an ordinary person. His confidences were given to Yaunie without any reserve. First, he suggested inveigling the raiders from S——'s vessel to his own, getting them down below and filling them full of champagne or whisky, whichever they preferred; and in the event of their remaining on board his friend's ship, they were to be made drunk there, and that being accomplished, the vessel was to be unmoored and taken to sea with them aboard, and they were to be landed or cast adrift in an open boat. The recital of these dare-devil propositions caused Yaunie's face to wear a careworn look, and when asked what he thought of it he said—

"Well, I try to tink, bit it is impossible. You speak what cannot happen. If you do what you say, how can you come back here? No, no; that must not be. I have better plan. No trouble, no get drunk, no run off with officers, no put him in boat; but leave it me: I settle everyting, suppose trouble come."

"Agreed again, old cockaloram. I'm only saying what I'd do. As I said before, you can do as you like, but I prefer giving these fellows 'what cheer!' I says again, what business have they to interfere with Englishmen carryin' on their business in their own way? I say they had no right to put a blockade on, and England should see that her subjects are duly protected."

This eloquent pronouncement of patriotism, with comic gesture added, excited the fiery dissent of the critical Levantine.

"Yes!" he retorted; "you tink everyting foreign should be for English. You swagger off with other people's country and say, 'This mine.' You like old J——b and G——d; they speak all the time same as you. English, English, everyting English! an' I say what for you stay? I Greek, an' I stay because Russia better for me."

This was said partly in jest and partly in good-natured earnestness, for Yaunie was a student of English characteristics. Farquarson explained that he would have to go to the Custom-house, and then to see his agents. Yaunie, with a significant look and gesture, warned him not to speak too much to port officers, bade him good-morning, said he would call back again in the afternoon, jumped on to the stage and went ashore.

It was late in the afternoon before Captain S—— got down to the docks. His steamer was loaded and ready for sea. At the quay, close to the stern of the vessel, Mrs. C——, with her daughter, was seated in a drosky. She explained that they had come to say good-bye, and to convey a message from Patrovish that he, Yaunie, and some officers were aboard Captain Farquarson's vessel. "He commissioned me to say that you were to slip out of the harbour quietly to avoid trouble, as he had reason to believe that there was something going on, and you might be stopped. Meanwhile, they are doing some entertaining for your benefit, so I will not detain you longer. Good-bye, and we hope to see you again soon."

The captain made haste aboard, and gave instructions to cast off the moorings. The *Claverhouse* glided quietly out of the harbour, and in less than an hour she was steaming fall speed towards the Bosphorus. The two captains did not meet again for several months, and when they did, Farquarson gave a vivid account of the development and ultimate success of what he termed the plot to extricate S—— from the possibility of being detained or heavily fined.

"I assure you," said he, "they were on the scent. They asked if I was the man who was on the gunboat when the English steamer ran over the mines. I swore by all that was holy that I didn't know what they were talking about. Then Yaunie and Patrovish asked them in Russian to have some refreshment aboard my ship, and they kicked up a devil of a row when they found you had gone without saying good-bye. Yaunie swore it was to cheat the pilotage, and Patrovish said he couldn't have believed it of you. I said you always were a bowdikite, and that you were putting on 'side.' The Russians were very jolly. They had a thimbleful or two of whisky, which made them talk a lot. We had a good laugh after they went away, and Patrovish said it was a good job you were gone, because they would have been sure to have caused trouble. Yaunie wasn't sure, but I was on C——'s side, for, I said, why did they mention the gunboat to me, if they didn't mean anything?"

"Whatever their intentions were," rejoined Captain S——, "the precautions you took to checkmate were successful, and I am much obliged for the trouble you took after you realized the danger. I must always be grateful to you for that; and the next time you go out there, thank my two friends for their important share in it, and say to Patrovish that his own and his wife's wish to see me soon back is much appreciated, but my present plans are such that I will not be able to visit Russia for a long time to come, and it may be I never shall again."

FOOTNOTES

[1] How came it to pass that the Russians were allowed to cross the Balkans? How was it that they were allowed to take possession so easily of the Schipka Pass? Did the personages who so soon afterwards disappeared mysteriously and were never heard of again yield up this stronghold to the possessors of a golden key? Poor Turkey!

Fair Trade and Foul Play

Smuggling at the beginning of the nineteenth century, and right up to the middle of it, was rampant, and was regarded as a wholesome profession by those who carried it on. They called it "fair trade," and looked upon those whose duty it was to destroy it with an aversion that oftentimes culminated in murderous conflict. The seafaring portion of this strange body of men, in characteristic contrast to their "landlubber" accomplices, never at any time, or under any circumstances, tried to conceal what their profession was. They were proud to be known as smugglers; whereas their shore colleagues, many of whom were gentry, or offshoots from it, adopted every possible means to turn suspicion from themselves when the preventive men were on the scent. Smugglers of that day were adroit tacticians; they had their signs just as Freemasons or any other craft have theirs. The pursuit was exciting, and the romance of it attracted men and women of gentle as well as of humble birth into its ranks. The men who manned the luggers were sailors who knew every bay and nook round the coast. They made heroic speeches expressive of their contempt for death. They talked boldly of powder magazines, and of blowing themselves and any one else up who put them into a tight corner; and there are instances on record that this was actually done. Be that as it may, they had great organizing skill and not a little business ability, whilst in their combination of strategy and valour they were unsurpassed. In many ways they were akin to pirates, though it could never be said that they went outside their own particular business— *i.e.*, they were not predatory buccaneers who murdered first and plundered afterwards. They believed, as I have said, their calling to be as legitimate as any other form of trading. Their doctrine was that it was the Government that acted illegally, and not themselves. It was not surprising, therefore, that the system should take so long a time to wipe out, notwithstanding the rigid way in which the whole coastline of the British Isles was guarded. Much has been written about the desperate ways of these men, but no accurate estimate can be formed by the present generation of the extent of the system, and the methods adopted to carry it on. Romance has gone far, but rarely too far, in describing it; and to really know it as it was you must have lived in its atmosphere, or have taken part, either for or against, in its attractions. One of the greatest ambitions of my early boyhood days comes to me now.

I had resolved that when I grew up I would secretly leave my home and join some smuggling lugger. Happily for me, the luggers had disappeared before I grew up.

Here is an authentic instance of professional attachment and pride. When I was quite a small boy a brig ran on to the rocks beneath my father's house. The captain was a fine, rollicking, sailorly-looking man, with a fascinating manner. He often came to our house during his stay in the locality, and one of the first things he told my parents was that in his younger days he was a smuggler, and had had many encounters with Deal coastguards. He spoke sadly of the way the "trade" was ruined by Government intervention, and said that he had never been really settled or happy since he was driven out of the business, and had to take service in the merchant navy for a living. He was asked if he would like to go back to it again.

"Go back to it again!" said he; "I wish I could! There is nothing to fill its place in the whole world. But that is done for now. Oh! what good money we used to make, and what narrow squeaks we had of being captured or killed."

It seems incredible that so great a change should have taken place in so short a time, considering that these sea-rovers were so firmly persuaded that their profession was as lawful as any other, and that they were persecuted and hounded to death by a set of whippersnappers who made insufferable laws! The system became so gigantic in the early part of last century that the Government had to appeal to the Navy, and a large number of officers and men were landed on the coast of Kent and Sussex, where a strict blockade was enforced. Later, a semi-civilian force under the control of the Customs was formed. This was called the "Preventive Water Guard," and subsequently it went under the new title of "Preventive Coastguard." The duties were arduous and risky. The men never went forth unless armed with a big dagger-stick and a flint-lock pistol, both of which were not infrequently used with effect. Owing to the dangerous character of the occupation, a high wage and pension was offered as an inducement to join the service; at least, the wage and pension were considered very good at the time. The men, however, rarely had decent houses to live in. Their uniform was rather like that of a naval officer. They would have disdained wearing the garb of the present-day coastguard. Their training in most cases consisted in service aboard a Revenue cutter for a few months before being appointed to a station. Many of these men were tradesmen who had never been to sea at all, and often were men of education and sterling character. For the most part these educated men were Wesleyans—or "Ranters," as they were called—and not a few were local preachers, and some of them were well versed in theology. They were stationed usually eight miles apart, right along the coast, and their ordinary duty was to meet each other half-way and exchange despatches. This gave the religious section opportunities of comparing experiences and discussing the faith that was in them. I knew one who spoke and taught French and Latin, another who could make an accurate abstract of Bishop Butler's *Analogy* from cover to cover, and another who became possessed of a small schooner, which made him a fortune while he was still in the service. The wives of these three coastguardsmen were quite as well informed and as ardent religionists as themselves, and took a common interest in books, educational matters, and in each other's home affairs. Their homes were always neat and clean, and the children were disciplined into a rigid, methodical life. It is a remarkable fact that the sons of each of these men have all risen to high positions in commerce, literature, art, and politics, and those that still survive are proud to acknowledge that they owe their position to the splendid example and beautiful home-life which they were taught to live when children. Guarding the coast was not the only occupation of the Preventive Coastguard.

There arose in 1848 a manning difficulty in the Navy, which became so grave that the large force of disciplined men employed in protecting the revenue were drilled in gunnery to fit them for sea service. Many of them were called out to serve aboard ship during the war with Russia in 1854. One of the grievances in the service was the irritating and unfair policy of the Board of Customs in constantly moving the men from one station to another. In many instances the hardships constituted a public scandal. Adequate recompense was never made for this breaking-up of their little homes, and frequently when they arrived at some outlandish coast village there was no provision made for housing them. I know of several instances where families were beholden to the generosity of the villagers or farmers for lodgings until a house was found. During the interval their furniture was stored in some dirty stable or store. It was not an uncommon thing for these poor fellows to be removed, with their families, from one end of England to the other two or three times in a year, at the behest of an uneasy bureaucratic commander-in-chief who knew little, and probably cared less, about the domestic hardships incurred. From Holy Island or Spital to Deal in those days of transit by sea was a greater and more hazardous voyage than that of Liverpool to New York to-day. The following story may give some idea of their life as they then lived it.

A group of fishermen stood at the north end of the row, watching a smart cutter that was beating from the north against a strong S.S.E. wind and heavy sea, which broke heavily on the beach and over an outlying reef of rocks which forms a natural breakwater and shelters the fishermen's cobles from the strong winds that blow in from the sea during the winter months. The cutter tacked close in to the north end of the ridge several times during the forenoon. Her appearance was that of a Government vessel, and her commander evidently wished to communicate with the shore. When the ensign was hoisted to the main gaff, the onlookers knew that she did not belong to the merchant service. The simple people who inhabited this district were concerned about the intentions of what they regarded as a mysterious visitor, and the firing of a small cannon from the taffrail did not lessen their perplexity. At last the national flag was hauled up and down, and the squire, who had come from his mansion amongst the woods, told the fishermen that those aboard the cutter were really asking for a boat to be sent to them.

The flood tide had covered the rocks. A volunteer crew of five fine specimens of English manhood were promptly got together, and a large coble was wheeled down the beach and launched into the breaking sea. They struggled with accustomed doggedness until they had passed the most critical part of the bay and got safely within speaking distance of the vessel. Two good-looking fellows in naval uniform stood on the quarter-deck, and one of these, the commander, asked the fishermen to take one of his officers ashore. To this they readily agreed, though they said it would be most difficult to land, as it was much safer to go off than come in, but they would risk that. The officer jumped into the boat, the rope was slipped, and then commenced a struggle between the endurance and skill of the hardy fishermen on the one hand and the angry cross seas which threatened to toss the boat and its occupants to destruction on the other. The officer suggested that the reefs should be let out of the sail to rush her over the dangerous corner of the entrance.

"I have used this plan often," said he, "and it always succeeded."

The coxswain demurred, although these men are very skilled in the handling of their boats; but at last he was prevailed upon by his crew to allow the officer to try the experiment. The latter only agreed to do so on condition that he was in no way interfered with, and his orders were strictly carried out. Up went the close-reefed lug; the occupants were instructed to lie low to windward, the men at the main sheet were ordered in a quiet, cool manner to ease off and haul in as necessity required. In a few minutes they had reached the crucial point. The men began to express anxiety, when amid the shrill song of the wind and the noise of the breaking seas, the man now in charge called out with commanding vigour—

"Steady your nerves, boys! I know quite well how to handle her."

The helmsman had barely finished his appeal when the combers began to curl up in rapid succession; the mass of water threatened to overwhelm the rushing craft, but she was manipulated with such fine seamanship that only the spray lashed over her in smothering clouds. Suddenly orders were given to stand by to lower the sail, and in another minute the helm was put down to bring the boat head to sea and wind. The sail was lowered, oars shipped, and she was manoeuvred stern on to the beach. As soon as she struck, a rush to help was made by those who had watched with feverish anxiety the passage through the broken water, lest the frail craft should be overturned and all aboard drowned. A rope was bent on to the stern, and the crowd quickly hauled the coble away from the heavy surf into safety. At this point, an elderly gentleman, tall, with a long, shaggy beard and bushy grey hair, which might have been a wig, rode up on a brown mare. His appearance and demeanour stamped him with the characteristics of a real old country gentleman, who put on what sailors would call an insufferable amount of "side." He promptly introduced himself to the officer as the Lord of the Manor, giving his name as Crawshaw.

The naval man gave his as Thomas Turnbull, and explained that he was sent to organize some system of resistance to the smuggling that was being carried on along that part of the coast. Mr. Crawshaw volunteered assistance, and hinted that the task would be rendered all the more arduous as he would not only have the smugglers to deal with, but their accomplices, the fisher-folk and farmers. After a few weeks' experience, it was quite obvious that the squire was right, and in view of this, Thomas Turnbull sent for his wife and six children, and settled down to his work in real earnest.

The intimation that the new-comer was a religious man, and could preach and pray, soon spread through the villages, and large numbers flocked to see and hear him. Many came out of pure curiosity, and some to mock and jeer, but these seldom succeeded in setting at defiance the great power that was behind the preacher. He was of commanding presence; his face, as some of the villagers used to say, was good to look at, and the message that he delivered to his audience came with irresistible force, which broke the spirit of some of the most determined obstructers, and turned many into friends, and a few even into saints. The fisher-folk did not take kindly to him, and so strong was their opposition that they threatened many times to take his life. Their savage ignorance would have unnerved and discouraged a less powerful personality, but this man seemed to be buoyed up by his belief that it was God's work and he was only the instrument in carrying it out. He was often warned of the violence that was threatened towards him, but the intimation never disturbed his inherent belief that no earthly power could break through the cordon that protected him; and so he continued his work, temporal and spiritual, undisturbed by the threats of a class whom he was determined to civilize, and, "with God's help, Christianize." The process was long, the methods of resistance wicked.

Jimmy Stone, one of the worst scoundrels in the district, had laboured to persecute Turnbull, and to break up the meetings for months past. He tyrannized over men and brutally maltreated women, and his blasphemy was terrible to listen to. It was during one of his outbursts of wrath against the "Ranter" preacher that he was suddenly staggered by Turnbull going up to him, laying his hand on his shoulder, and admonishing him to refrain from such shocking conduct. He attempted to seize the preacher by the throat, and I fear at this juncture Turnbull forsook for a little his usual attitude of equanimity, for before the giant knew where he was he lay on the ground, stunned by a left-hander. The preacher was an awkward customer to deal with, and it would seem as though he did not entirely trust to Divine interposition when hands were laid on him. His tormentor lay, a humiliated heap, at his feet. Never in Jimmy's life had any one dared to resent his attacks in this way. He could not understand it, and was overcome more by superstition and a fear of Turnbull's reputed supernatural aids than by real fear of his physical powers. Turnbull ordered the bully to stand up, and warned him against experimenting on strangers. He then, in quaint, old-world phraseology, the outcome of much deep reading of Butler, Baxter, and Jeremy Taylor, and wholly without cant or affectation, went on to say—

"I intend to let you off lightly on this occasion, but if I hear of you practising any injustice or in any way giving annoyance to your neighbours again, I shall deem it my duty to teach you a salutary lesson. Now, bear in mind what I say to you; and remember that the Almighty may visit you with His wrath. It may be that He will send to your house affliction, and even make it desolate by taking some one from you whom you love. Or He may see that the only way of checking the course of your wickedness is to have you laid aside with sickness. It is probable that He will smite you by taking away from your evil influence some of your children. God is very merciful to little children when they are in the hands of brutes like you. Go away from me! and ponder over what I have said."

Jimmy slouched off, muttering vengeance against the Almighty if He dared to interfere with his bairns, and, as an addendum, he vividly portrayed the violent death of Turnbull. He slunk listlessly into his cottage, tumbled on to a seat, and was lost in meditation. Jenny, his wife, tremulously asked what ailed him. She was alarmed at his subdued manner; she had never known him come into the house without bullying and using blasphemous language to her and the children, and oftentimes this was accompanied by blows that well-nigh killed her and them; and yet she stood loyally by him whenever he needed a friend. Suddenly he jumped to his feet, and as though he had become possessed of an inspiration, broke silence by vigorously exclaiming to his wife that he had settled the manner of the "Ranter" preacher's death.

"Aa'll catch him some neet betwixt here and the burn [stream], and finish him. That'll stop his taak aboot the Almighty takin' ma bairns frae me!"

Jimmy's idea was that Turnbull was in communion with the Almighty for the removal of his children, and if he were put out of the way there would be an end to it. Jenny was no less ignorant than her husband, and therefore no less superstitious about meddling with this mysterious person who had come amongst them and wrought such extraordinary changes in the lives of many of her class. She doubted the wisdom of killing the preacher, as she had heard that these people lived after they were killed, and might wreak more terrible vengeance when their lives assumed another form. She urged her husband to leave well alone; not because she in any way differed from his views in regard to Turnbull's preaching and his attitude generally towards evil-doers, or objected to his being put to death; but she preferred some person other than her husband should do it. Hence, she disagreed with his policy, and he in turn raged at her for taking sides against him.

"This interloper's spyin' into everythin' we dee and say," said he. "We had nee taak aboot religion afore he cum, and noo there's nowt but religion spoken, so that we can hardly get a man or a woman t' dee any trootin' inside the limit; an' when we dee get a chance we hev t' put wor catches into th' oven, for feor him or his gang gan sneakin' aboot and faal in wi' summat they hae nee reet t' see. Forbye that, within the last few months he's driven the smugglers off the coast, and deprived us o' monny an honest soverin' in helpin' them t' and theor stuff. And then he's got the gob t' tell me that if aa divvent change me ways, the Almighty'll dee God knaw's what tiv us! He'll myek sickness cum, and mebbies tyek sum o' th' bairns frae us. It'll be warse for him if harm cums t' th' bairns, or me either! Aa tell't him that this mornin', an' aa said he might tell his Almighty that he taaked see much aboot, if he liked."

Jenny secretly disapproved of carrying retaliation any further, but dared not openly say another word in favour of her views, for, as she afterwards said, "Aa was afeared ye might kill me afore ye got a chance o' killin' the preacher."

Mr. Turnbull knew what Jimmy's intentions were, and purposely put himself in his way, so that he might say a cheery word to him in passing; but he never got more than a grunt in response. He knew that this wild creature was in league with a gang of the most desperate smugglers that the "Preventer men" had to contend with. No landing, however, had been seriously attempted during the time that Turnbull had been at the station. Craft had been sighted and signals exchanged, and then the suspected craft disappeared for weeks. The men who guarded the coast knew these buccaneers had emissaries, and could have laid hands on them, but preferred to catch them red-handed.

After weeks of close watching and waiting, information was passed along the coast that a landing would take place close to the spot where Turnbull now lived with his wife and children. Men from all the stations extending over a radius of fifty miles were summoned to meet at a certain point at eleven o'clock on a certain night. Trusted civilians had been drafted into the service for the occasion; and so accurate was the information given, that within a couple of hours of the time several boat-loads of contraband were landed above high-water mark. Three carts came along, and while the process of transhipping into them was going on, the "Preventer" men, led by Turnbull, quietly came from their concealment, and with a sudden rush surrounded the smugglers. Those of their accomplices who had smelt the scent of battle fled behind the hills, and got clean away. One of the carts attempted to bolt, but a shower of shot targeted into the horses peremptorily stopped that move, and the drivers were easily captured. The smugglers fought like polecats, but received no help from the few accomplices who had not escaped. These, either from fear or policy, or both, did not attempt to extricate themselves or lend their support to a lost cause. It was common knowledge that smugglers drew lots as to who had to escape if severe fighting or capture became inevitable, and the battle became the more fierce in order to cover the escape of those few. They did not all succeed in getting off in their boat, but it was estimated half a dozen might have done so. The rest, something like a score, were ultimately overpowered, sent to prison and tried in the good old style, and sentenced to transportation to the criminal dumping-ground of Western Australia.

The notorious Jimmy Stone on that memorable moaning night was disguised, but that did not prevent him being detected while rendering assistance to land and convey the contraband on to the beach and into the carts. One of the Government men was indiscreet enough to shout "James Stone, you are my prisoner!" and almost before the words were out of his mouth Jimmy dropped a keg of gin on to him and fled. The companions of the stunned man were too busy with the other cut-throats to follow Jimmy, or to see in what direction he had gone. It was only after the conflict was over that they were reminded that this lawless fisherman had escaped, and must at all costs be captured and brought to justice. A party was selected to search for him. They knew that he must be hiding in some of the hollows where the thick clusters of bents and bracken would give him cover. Some of the party had strayed from the central group, and were talking of Jimmy's prowess and astuteness, and wondering where he was concealed, when they suddenly came across a man with his head and part of his body up a rabbit-hole. He was asking in subdued tones, "Are the — — gyen yet?" and one of the party, in the same tone of voice and the same dialect and language as he had used, cautioned him not to speak too loud, as they were still hovering about.

"My God!" said he, "when aa get oot o' this mess aa'll hae ma revenge on that Ranter." And becoming impatient, he began to curse at his supposed friend for advising him to put his head in a rabbit-hole, vigorously announcing that he wished his — — head was there instead of his own. "Aa cud hae run if ye hadn't persuaded me t' hide heor."

"Hae patience!" responded the voice from without.

"Patience be d— —!" said he; "Aa wish aa had them— — Government men heor. Aa wad make short work o' them, the — — rascals!"

"Whisht," said his companion; "they're comin' this way!"

In a few seconds Jimmy's posterior became the subject of some vigorous thrashing. He was dragged, yelling, from his retreat, and confronted with the men he had so recently sworn to murder. They asked if he was Jimmy Stone. He replied in the affirmative, and added—

"Aa thowt it was Jack Dent aa was taakin' tee. He cum heor wiv us."

"Where is he now?" inquired the officer.

"Hoo am aa t' knaa?" said Jimmy; "but the Lord help him when aa dee cum across him. He's betrayed me. Nivvor more will aa put me heed in a rabbit-hole!"

His soliloquy was cut short by his captors putting his hands in irons and conveying him to where their colleagues were; and Jimmy would have been included amongst the convicts but for the magnanimous intercession of Turnbull, who informed his captors that they were to leave Jimmy to him. He was working out a scheme whereby his knowledge would be invaluable to the Service. So James was not sent to the Colonies.

A well-known farmer, who was accustomed to make friendly calls on the Turnbull family, was caught in the act of bolting with a cartload of unlawful merchandise. He was sent to Australia, but not as a convict. Turnbull had found some useful purpose for him also, and he was advised to get out of the country, lest it became too hot for him.

A couple of ladies had attracted special attention; not that they were bellicose, but because in consequence of their abnormal bulk they created some suspicion that they had concealed beneath their crinolines more than their ordinary form. They were asked unchivalrously to undo their clothing, and with comic dignity and superb self-possession they defiantly declined. They were then told in the name of the Queen that if they did not undress voluntarily it would have to be done for them, whereupon they adopted the old dodge of weeping and calling themselves unprotected women, whose characters were being assailed by men whom it was not safe for females to be amongst, making the sandy hollows resound with their artificial shrieks and sobs; but it was all to no purpose. Their skirts were examined, and there were found boxes of cigars, packets of tobacco, and bottles of gin, all hooked in methodical order to an ingenious arrangement connected with the skirt. These ladies were proved to be on familiar terms with the red-capped gentlemen who were defrauding the Revenue, and not infrequently shooting down its guardians.

One of these women was the sister of Jimmy Stone, and the other his wife, and it would have gone hard with them had Turnbull not conceived the humane idea of reclaiming and ultimately drafting them into the Service. He convinced his colleagues that they would be invaluable adjutants. They would take a deal of taming, as there was little to distinguish them from a species of wild animal. He requested that they should be handed over to him for the purpose of trying the experiment. The women and Jimmy were locked up in separate rooms in the Old Tower for a week. Turnbull visited them daily, and detected on each visit the growth of penitence; his little talks had penetrated their stony, vicious natures, until at last they broke down and humbly solicited pardon and release, which was granted under well-defined conditions. There was much talk in the village about the leniency extended to the fishers. Tom Hitchings, the cartman, declared that they should have been sent to the Colonies, the same as the other smugglers; and Ted Robson said transportation was too good a punishment, they ought to have been shot or bayonetted, and had any other person but a ranter preacher been in charge it would have been done.

"How de we knaa, Tom," said Ted, "that them fiends o' smugglers winnot rise oot o' theor beds in the deed hoor o' the neet and break into wor homes and cut wor throats afore we're awake? We helped te catch them, whaat for shouldn't we hev some say aboot theor punishment?"

"That's whaat aa says," replied Tom. "But ye'll heor o' some queer things happenin' varry syen. He'll be hevvin' his meetin's in Jenny's hoose, and Jimmy'll be preachin' afore lang. Ther'll be fine scenes if it's not throttled i' the bud."

"Get away, man," said Ned; "they're the biggest blackguards roond the countryside, and they'll steal, rob, or morder, whichivver comes handiest. What d'ye think that fellow Jimmy did once? A ship was in the offin'. She had distress signals flyin'. He could get neebody te man a boat but women; the men wadn't hev onythin' te dee wiv him, so his awn wife, Ailsie's Jenny, Nanny Dent, and Peggy Story went. They pulled the boat through monster seas, and the brute was cursin' at the women aal the way until they gat alangside, when the captain said, 'Ma ship's sinkin'.' The crew were telled to jump into the boat smart, and as syen as the captain said, 'We're aal heor,' Jimmy sprang aboard like a cat, cast the boat adrift, shooted to his wife, 'She's mine! Pull the — — ashore, and then come off and we'll take her in!' The captain saa the trick and demanded to be taken back, but Jenny felled him with the tiller, and threatened to slay onny of the others. They were nearly ashore when the captain exclaimed, 'She's not his; Sancho, the dog, has been left behind!' The crew were landed, and the boat went back to the ship. The women gat aboard, and asked Jimmy if he had seen a dog. He said, 'There's nee dog heor; the ship's wors,' and they say he fand the dog on the floor and that he put it ower-board. Now, there's a born convict for ye! An' they tell me, him and his women gat the ship safely into port, and the folk shooted, 'Bravo, Jimmy Stone!' They said he was a hard swearer, but a brave, clever fellow, and aa said when aa hard it, 'Whaat aboot the dog?' The ship was selled, and Jimmy gat summit — whaat de they caal it — salvage, aa think. They say he's worth lots o' money."

"But whaat did they say aboot the dog?" said Tom.

"Wey, the captain said the dog was left as a safeguard against bein' boarded and claimed as a derelict; but Jimmy swore that the dog wasn't there when he gat aboard, and neebody saa what becam' on't, and so the matter rests. They often say te him, 'Whe tossed the dog ower board?' and aa believe he's nearly mordered half a dozen big men for sayin' sic things."

"Eh, man," said Tom pensively, "what a grand Christian gentleman he'll make!"

Shortly after Jimmy's release from the Old Tower, his youngest child succumbed to the ravages of a malignant fever. He and his wife were distracted, as, in spite of their pagan instincts and habits, their devotion to their offspring was a passion. They remembered Mr. Turnbull appealing to them to flee from the wrath to come by amending their ways, lest something terrible befell themselves or their children, and instead of the recollection of this warning kindling strong demonstrations of resentment against the lay preacher now, Jenny implored her husband to run over the moor and get Mr. Turnbull to come and administer comfort to them.

"He'll give us the sacrament, and pray for us at the bedside were the deed bairn lies."

Jimmy was dazed at the suggestion. He could not quite bring himself to give up the idea of some day renewing his former habits of aiding the smugglers, and of doing a bit of poaching. He was quite frank in stating to his wife that he feared if Turnbull came and prayed with them he would get him to join the chapel folk, and there would be no more poaching or smuggling after that.

"And see what a loss it wad be tiv us. But," said he, "to tell the truth, aa hev been for prayin' mesel ever since the bairn tuck bad, but then aa thowt it was cowardly to ask help when aa was in difficulties and nivvor at ony other time. So I didn't dee 't."

Jenny interjected that at the risk of being led to join the Methodists, and throwing over all thought of joining in any more lawlessness, he must go to the village and ask Mr. Turnbull to come.

"I feel somethin' forcin' me to this, Jimmy; so get away and be quick back."

And as James felt the same throbbing impulse, off he went, and within an hour presented his petition to Mr. Turnbull, who received him in his usual kind way, which caused the redoubtable ruffian to melt into tears, and volubly to confess all his murderous intentions towards the man he now believed to be the only agency on earth that could give him comfort.

The two men started at once for the bereaved home. The first part of the journey was tramped in solemn meditation. At last Jimmy broke silence by asking his companion if he thought God had taken his child from him as a punishment for his sins. Turnbull said—

"Well, James, I believe your heavenly Father has some work for you to do. He has often warned you of the wrath to come by confronting you with danger at sea; and only a short time since you were caught in the act of committing a crime, and narrowly escaped being banished to a penal settlement, and He mercifully used a friend as an instrument to save you from this degradation. But you still maintained the spirit of defiance, and were a law unto yourself. The Almighty saw that drastic measures would have to be taken to break down your wilful opposition. Your child was stricken with illness, and still you went on cursing God and man; and then in His wondrous compassion for you and hundreds of other men and women to whom I believe He has planned you shall carry the message of peace, He has taken your child in order that you may be saved. He knew that was the only way of bringing you to see the great plan of salvation, and to save your innocent little girl from growing up in a heathenish home, where there was no beauty, no kindness, no good example, no God. I beseech you to surrender yourself at once. Remember, the Spirit will not always strive with you, and if you chase it away now it may never return."

That night, kneeling by the side of his dead child, Jimmy implored God to be merciful to him, and professed to have experienced the great transition from death unto life. Now, Jimmy, though quite uneducated, had an intellectual head and great natural gifts, and when he was careful he spoke with amazing correctness. He commenced to take part in the prayer meetings at once, and having a good memory, he picked up all the stock phrases and used them vigorously. Being an apt pupil, he soon learned to read, and then commenced one of the most extraordinary religious campaigns that has ever been witnessed in that part of Great Britain. Hundreds of men and women were led to change their lives by this rugged, uncultured, but natural preacher. A certain number of his own class viciously persecuted him for years, and none more so than his own wife. It seemed as though Hell had been let loose on him, and yet he went on undisturbed, steadfastly believing that he was the agent of the living God to carry the message of truth to the heathen. His old enemy Turnbull had become his fast friend, from whom he sought and received much help and many acts of kindness. He owed the conversion of his wife and many of his persecutors to this spiritually-minded man, and it was remarkable that nearly all the worst characters who were "brought in" opened their doors whenever he wanted to have a prayer meeting or a preaching service, and the rooms were always packed with people.

Attracted by the originality of the converted fisherman, a few young people belonging to the better families in the locality gathered together to witness what they imagined would be mere burlesque. There was only standing room behind the kitchen bed for them, and there was anything but an air of sanctity amongst that portion of his congregation. Jimmy's pulpit style was peculiar. He was flashing out eloquent phrases that were not commonly used in the orthodox pulpit. As he warmed to his work he broke out in rhyme—"Yes, brothers and sisters, there was little brother Paal, the very best of aal, laid down his life," etc. His use of biblical names was quite eccentric, which caused the undevotional members of his audience to snigger audibly. Without seeming to heed the irreverence, Jimmy pursued his impassioned diatribe and smote unbelievers hip and thigh, in language that was not conventional, or even relevant to the subject of his discourse. The sniggering had developed into suppressed laughter, and James suddenly stopped the even flow of his oratory, brought his giant fist down on the deal table and sent everything flying. Ladies' dresses were more or less damaged by candle grease; but the cooler heads prevented an outbreak of panic by getting the candles relighted and put on to the table. Then in reverent tones they asked the preacher, who stood apparently unmoved, to proceed with the service; so Jimmie gave out the verse of a hymn which he thought would be suitable to the occasion. (Methodists always did that when the lights went out or the preacher stuck.)

In the good old days, when village Methodism was quivering with spiritual life, and pouring its converts into the cities and towns of England to teach the simple gospel of the Founder of our Faith, without any artificial fringes being attached to it, they were too poor, and perhaps too conscious of the superiority of the real God-given vocal capacity, to have anything to do with what many of them believed to be artificial aids to religion. It was a fine sight to see the leader of the songsters shut his eyes, clap his hands, and with strong nasal blasts—which resembled the drone of the immortal instrument that is the terror of the English and the glory of the Scottish people—"raise the hymn," while, as the others joined in the singing, the volume of sound swelled louder and louder, until the whole congregation were entranced by the power of their own performance.

I give the words of the verse which Jimmy asked to be sung. Here they are—

> "Come on, my partners in distress,
> My comrades through the wilderness,
> Who still your bodies feel;
> Awhile forget your griefs and fears,
> And look beyond this vale of tears
> To that celestial hill."

This was sung with appropriate vigour over and over again. It is very difficult to stop a real country Methodist when the power of song is on him, and on occasions such as this they generally break off gradually, until only one or two irrepressible enthusiasts are left singing, and these have to be brought to the consciousness of time and the propriety of things by being pulled down into their seats. Jimmy wished to proceed with his rebuke to the persons who had been the cause of the diversion, so he put a peremptory stop to the vocalists by telling them to "sit doon, and listen to God's ambassador." He then resumed his address by stating that when his fist knocked the candles off the table he was "nearly givin' way to temptation. In fact," said he, "I was just on the point of usin' profane language to the mockers and scoffers of the sarvent of the livin' God. I mean them parvarse lads and lasses aback o' the bed theor."

"Amen!" interjected several saintly voices.

"But, hallelujah!" resumed James, "aa felt God was ha'd'en me back!"

"Glory!" shouted Adam Jefferson.

"Yes, ma brethren and sistors. Aa cum amang ye t' seek and t' save sinners that repenteth; rich or poor, it makes nee difference to me nor ma Maister, for hasn't He said 'where two or three are met tegithor in Ma Name, there am I in the midst'?"

"Bless Him!" cried Nannie Dent, a late accomplice of the smugglers.

Jimmy's rebuke to the offenders was delivered with boisterous earnestness, but the comic phrasing of it created irrepressible hilarity, and they had to leave the room. The preacher, in his closing remarks, reminded his hearers that he was once a black-hearted rascal, drinking, swearing, stealing, poaching, smuggling, and but for the mercy of God he might have added to his other crimes that of murder. A shudder went through the congregation when "murder" was uttered, and their minds were obviously centred on the derelict vessel and the dog, which Jimmy was suspected of doing away with.

"Ah!" whispered Sam Taylor, the butler, "he should never have ventured on that affair. Folks are varra queer, and whether it is true or not, they like sensation and scandal."

As though he had been gifted with prescience, Jimmy continued—"Aa can feel whaat ye are thinking aboot, but it's not true. This is the man aa threatened te kill," pointing at Turnbull. "And now let us bow oor heads in solemn, silent prayor for a few minutes, and ask forgiveness for oor past and daily sins. And aa want ye to join with me in asking for pardon and speedy repentance to be sent tiv a porson that belangs te the gentry of this district, but whe hes been, and is noo engaged in trafficking in wickedness. May the Lord bring him to His footstool of mercy before he is nabbed, as aa was."

These remarks, with the exhilarating petition, caused an amount of irreverent speculation as to who was the person alluded to. The service was brought to a close without any evidences of spiritual emotion such as had characterized previous meetings, and the people proceeded in groups to their respective homes filled with fertile curiosity, and a sinister suspicion as to who the sinful person was that Jimmy had so fervently prayed for. But only one person who heard the rugged deliverance fixed her mind on him that was guilty, and she resolved to keep her thoughts a secret, for reasons that will be explained hereafter. Meanwhile, many innocent men were suspected, and gossip ran rampant. Jimmy, when asked whom he meant, was piously reticent, and merely answered—

"That is a matter that concerns God and mysel'! The time may come when he'll accuse hissel'. Aa'm prayin' mornin', noon, and night, that the strings of his heart may be broken, and that a penitent condition of mind may take possession of him, and in the fulness of a new borth he may cry aloud, 'O Lord, once I was blind, noo I see!'"

When Thomas Turnbull and his wife arrived home, they found the younger members of their family in an excited state of hilarity. The youngest daughter was mimicking Jimmy perfectly, and had her brothers and sister in fits of laughter. Their father could not refrain from joining in the fun, but the mother was quiet and pensive, and got rather huffed when her husband chided her in his good-humoured way with being indifferent to the happy surroundings. Poor woman, she was troubled about Jimmy's prayer, and thought it irreligious to be joyous in the midst of such dark mystery.

The following afternoon, Mrs. Turnbull paid a visit to Mrs. Clarkson, who listened with eager interest to the account of the meeting, and when the words of the closing prayer were conveyed an anxious look came over her countenance, and she made an effort to change the subject, without, however, preventing Mrs. Turnbull from detecting her confusion.

"Let us talk of something else; I do not like," said she, "conversing about sensational things; it makes me nervous. And if I were you, I would try to forget what has been said to you about important personages being involved in lawless traffic. It will only make you unhappy, and serve no good purpose. If there is anything of the sort going on, it will be discovered, and those that are guilty will be brought to justice."

Mrs. Turnbull did not pursue the subject any farther, but the sad, pained look of her hostess became fixed in her memory. She could not shake the conviction from her that Mrs. Clarkson was haunted by the dread of some one belonging to herself having some connection with Jimmy's prayer.

Mrs. Turnbull paid frequent visits to the farm, and one winter evening she happened to be there when a violent snowstorm made the ground impassable, so she was prevailed upon to stay until the following day. The household consisted of Mrs. Clarkson, her sister, and two nieces, who were very pleased to have the company of a woman who was so full of information and reminiscence. Her mother was said to have been the daughter of a Scottish law-lord's son, who was disinherited because he was thought to have married beneath his station—that is, instead of marrying the lady selected by his father from his own class, who had nothing in common with him, he had chosen and fixed his affections on a lady outside his rank, who was talented, had high intellectual and religious qualities, and good looks, but was financially poor. Mrs. Turnbull had excited the curiosity of the two young ladies by relating this part of her history, and they were naturally eager to hear more. With that object in view, they asked their aunt to allow her to sleep in their room, and the request was granted. The good lady, however, had said all that she intended to say about herself, and notwithstanding the ingenious and persuasive requests of her young friends, she stood steadfastly to her resolve. She talked to them about the farm and their aunt and cousins, and her own family, and the religious work that was being carried on, but never another word about herself or her ancestry could be drawn from her. Perhaps it was that she considered it scarcely wise to discuss romance with young girls. And so they talked themselves out about other things, and then went to sleep.

Early in the morning, Mrs. Turnbull was awakened by what she took to be a door slamming. She got up with the intention of closing it, and then heard voices talking, sometimes in an ordinary tone, but for the most part in an excited whisper. She listened, with the bedroom door ajar, and heard the voice of Mrs. Clarkson say—

"If you do not dissociate yourself from these wicked men you will come to grief. You are supposed to be in Australia. Indeed, it may be that Mr. Turnbull has his suspicion even now that I am harbouring an accomplice of the men whose trade is smuggling, and who try to get rid of those who prevent them carrying it on. I beseech you to cut yourself adrift from that other man, who, I believe, has you under his influence, and who, I feel sure, is associated with this gang of lawbreakers."

At this stage, Mrs. Turnbull could not restrain the desire to cough. She did try to subdue it, but Mrs. Clarkson's companion whispered to her—

"Whist! I hear some one on the landing."

"Do not fear," said Mrs. Clarkson; "it is only the wind making noises through the trees."

But her companion knew better, so not another word was spoken.

The next morning Mrs. Clarkson looked worried, but she was quite affable with her guest, who acted her part without giving the slightest suspicion of having overheard the little nocturnal conversation.

Immediately after breakfast, Mrs. Turnbull bade farewell to the family, and was soon in the thick of domestic matters in her own home. That night's experience at the Dean Farm settled the destiny of several families. The information unwittingly gleaned and discreetly used, led to far-reaching consequences to the district, and to all those involved.

It was well known that the smugglers had places of concealment other than the accommodation gratuitously given them by certain farmers. The secret of the real cave's whereabouts was successfully kept, but one of those accidents that often come to disturb the current of human affairs led to an important discovery.

Softly the night wind blew over a glassy sea. The sound of the rippling water on the reef of rocks and on the sandy beach had a weird, melancholy effect. Then came the dull noise of muffled oars commingling with the cawing of the gull and hollow surging of the waters into the Fairy Rocks. There was neither moon nor stars visible, but in the bay the experienced eye could discern the mysterious lugger. There she lay, hove to, or anchored below the Dean House, which could be seen peeping out between two sandy hills. A dim light—which, to the uninformed, would have conveyed the impression of a light in a cottage window, but which was really a signal to the smugglers that the coast was clear—flickered in a line with the sandy valley; and, in truth, the quietude of the night betokened all was well. The landing was successfully made without interruption, and the men gaily entered on the task of transporting the cargo to its destination, believing, as they had a right to believe, that a big haul would be stored without a single hitch in the process. The accomplices scattered after their work was done, and the sailors returned to their vessel, no doubt well satisfied with the night's enterprise. But notwithstanding the many scouts they sent out, they were quite oblivious of the fact that their movements had been closely watched. Sail was set, and the sneaking craft crept out into the illimitable darkness, having apparently completed its work unseen by unfriendly eyes. There was not a little talk round the countryside about the landing that had taken place without any one in authority to check its progress. Wise, knowing people said it was timidity, and others attributed it to indifference to the public service; the truth being, it was neither the one nor the other. It was, in fact, a carefully-planned scheme to discover exactly where the mysterious cave was situated; and although in spite of exhaustive search the entrance to it could not be found, they had got a clue to its locality. A vigorous policy of exploration was inaugurated, but after many weeks of toil the operations were abandoned without the mystery having been penetrated. It was thought that time and opportunity would solve the problem, but how it was to be solved no one knew. There was, indeed, great speculation as to what might happen should another landing be attempted, but month after month passed without any indication of this, and the little population had settled down to a dull monotony. Except for a casual reference to the stirring times, the smugglers and their emissaries were apparently all but forgotten. The Preventive men were secretly as much on the alert as when the smugglers were most active. They purposely adopted an apparent indifference with the idea of luring the rovers into over-confidence. Each party took into account the possibility of being betrayed. In all secretive illegal societies there are suspects. Jimmy Stone having changed his mode of life, suspicion fell very naturally on him; but though he sometimes darkly hinted at the identity and the secrets of his late allies, he was never known to definitely divulge anything that would incriminate them. The nephew of Mrs. Clarkson was another marked man, as was also a friend of his. The former had been very little heard of in those parts since the night that his aunt implored him to give up his associates. The last that was really seen of Lawrence and his friend, they were drinking together in a public-house, and a few days after some of their torn and blood-stained clothes were found in a lonely hedged-in lane close by the moor. This dreaded place was called the "Mugger's Lonnin" by the country-folk, owing to its being a camping-ground for the gipsies, and from end to end it was prolific of bramble-berries and other wild fruit. When the children went during the summer months to gather these they were always accompanied by a few grown-up people, as it was believed that many terrible tragedies had happened there. The discovery of the clothes and the patches of blood right in the middle of the lonnin was indicative of a foul murder having taken place, and the bodies dragged along the grass to some place of concealment. Search parties were formed, bloodhounds were called into requisition, but no trace of the murdered lads' bodies could be found, and for many months this supposed terrible crime was sealed in mystery. A few people were callous enough to say that they were convinced that no murder had taken place, but these were very unpopular. The greater part of the small colony liked sensation, and nursed this one assiduously until an almost greater came to hand by it leaking out that the two men had been expeditiously sent to Australia, and that the blood on their clothes was not their own, but that of a sheep which had been killed for the purpose of misleading. This exciting revelation lead to important issues. Were they really alive and in Australia? Had they been bribed to reveal the secrets of their former friends, or was it dread of capture that caused them to be sent out of the country? These were some of the outspoken conjectures that flowed with ever-increasing imagination. The real facts never became known, but the tales of these stirring times have been handed down in more or less hyperbolic form. It may be fairly assumed that Thomas Turnbull got reliable information from some source which he was never known to disclose, and having got it, he hastened to use it judiciously and to advantage.

The entrance to the cave was at last found at a spot where he and his comrades had many times traversed. It was so ingeniously concealed that they might have searched until the day of doom, and it could never have been found but for the agency that conveyed him to the spot. Tradition speaks of it being a long subterranean passage, running east to west, and opening out close to a road that was quite accessible to carts. It was honeycombed with compartments, and so carefully were they constructed that only the initiated could have discovered their locality. Some of the cells still contained quantities of contraband, so that the Board of Customs made a good haul.

Turnbull frequently rubbed shoulders with men and women who eloquently declaimed against the smugglers and their allies. He knew these people were in the inner circle of the traffic. He realized also that it was not good policy to let them see that he knew that they were merely acting a part. He might some day have to make use of them. There was a section who never disguised their antipathy to him. They saw that through him the day of smuggling on that part of the coast was well-nigh over—if not over altogether. It was he who had been the instrument of emptying the vaults of treasure which they regarded as legitimately theirs, and closing them to further enterprise. It was, in fact, the system that he represented that was paralyzing their honest efforts of contributing to their means of subsistence! These were only some of the many indictments proclaimed against him and his colleagues. The aggrieved ones strolled about with an air of injured virtue, and their ferocious looks and veiled threats at the intruder as he passed along betokened the belief in their prescriptive right to plunder the Revenue. I think it is Macaulay who says that "no man is so merciless as he who is under a strong self-delusion."

The seizure of the storehouse gave a staggering blow to the "fair-traders," but it did not prevent them from making another desperate attempt to land their wares, and also to have their revenge by destroying a few of her Majesty's servants. On dark nights the horn lanterns were seen about the links, the flare-light flashed across the sea, and the curlew's shrill call was heard. These signs were now known to the Preventive staff; but they also had their signs and their means of conveying news, so that when the low, sneaking black lugger again appeared, they were ready for the fray.

There she was, snugly anchored in the sleepy bay. The first boat-load had left her side. The slow, dull sound of the horses' hoofs vibrated through the hollows, and the night wind from the fields of sleep blew softly over the rustling bents, causing a weird, peaceful lullaby. The boat's bow is run on to the beach, a dozen or more men jump from her into the water and haul her up as far as the weight of the cargo will allow. They then commence to discharge. Again the curlew's call is heard, again the sharp flare-light is seen; but no aid comes. The cargo is landed at high-water mark; they realize something is wrong, and hesitate whether to re-ship or re-embark without it. They are soon disillusioned. A horse gallops madly from the south. The rider shouts at the top of his voice, "Run, sailors, run! Treachery!" and then heads his horse full speed in the direction he came from, and is soon lost to view. The men push their boat into the sea, and row with all their might towards the vessel. Bullets from a score of muskets whiz over their heads; but they are accustomed to this, and lay their backs into the oars with increased vigour. Meanwhile, a coble sails almost peacefully alongside their ill-fated craft. In an instant a crowd of concealed men rush aboard and call out, "Surrender!" But smugglers were not given to surrender when merely requested, so a hand-to-hand fight took place. The butt-end of muskets were freely used, and to some purpose. There was no heroic effort to get at the powder magazine, so that they might blow themselves and everybody else up.

The lugger was in undisputed possession of the Revenue men before the boat from the shore reached her. They, too, were quickly disposed of, after a short, angry, though feeble resistance. Stringent precautions were taken to prevent any blowing-up exploits. The whole gang were well secured against that, and any other hostile outbreaks. This having been done to the satisfaction of the officer in charge, the anchor was weighed, a course was shaped towards the south, and the last of the low, black, romantic luggers, with their gallant crews, passed away, never more to be seen on this part of the coast.

Recognition of the deeds done by the dauntless heroes of that age in the Government service was very scanty. It may be they did not expect it. In that case they were rarely disappointed. Thomas Turnbull seems to have got his reward in being allowed to remain on the station until the time came to retire on a pension. He went about his routine work with placid regularity, and devoted what leisure he had to widening his reading, which consisted mainly of history, theology, and Burns's poems. He was never known to miss his class-meeting, and travelled eight miles each way to keep his pulpit appointments on Sundays. He sometimes entertained his family and the young folk that visited them by relating his experiences with the smugglers, but his greatest pleasure was in holding religious meetings in one or other of the fishers' cottages. In this he was gratuitously aided by Jimmy Stone, who entered into his work with energy, zeal, and oftentimes amazing resource. Jimmy had developed a form of religious mania, insisting on the theory that he was, as a preacher, a direct descendant of the Apostles. This assumption severely taxed the Christian virtues of the little society. Turnbull, who had a keen sense of humour, viewed the new situation with intense amusement, and always excused the foibles of his old convert up to the time of leaving the district to end his own eventful career within easy reach of his family, who were all grown-up and doing well. Jimmy did not long survive him, but he lived long enough to see the passing away of that spiritual wave that had changed his whole life.

Many years after, an ugly incident broke the spell of monotony in the village. A hideous-looking creature came to it and addressed himself to a fisherman. His voice was that of a drunkard. He was dirty, his eyes were bleared, and the cunning, shifty look betokened a long life of vicious habits. He wished to know when Mrs. Clarkson died, where all her relations that lived round about her were, to whom the estates were sold, and whom the money they realized went to; what had become of Turnbull and his family, and how long was it since the smugglers were driven off the coast? These questions were only meagrely answered, as the man he inquired of belonged to another generation, and there were only very few left who knew anything of the period or the people that he desired information about. The following day the body of a man, supposed to be a tramp, was found in a barn. He had left evidence of his identity, and when it was discovered that the stranger was Stephen Lawrence, Mrs. Clarkson's nephew, the once flashy young gentleman who controlled her estates, and who had been sent abroad when grave suspicion rested upon him of being seriously involved in pecuniary defalcations, it created a fresh sensation, and revived all the old stories of bygone days. He had come to die within the shadow of the home in which he was so indulgently reared, and his remains were buried by those who knew not of him. It was probably through him and Melbourne that the secret locality of the cave and other valuable information which led up to the final conflict and defeat of the smugglers became known.

The "Mugger's Lonnin," all blazing with red and yellow flowers and long silvery grass growing wild, and covering the mysteries that lie beneath, is still there. The superstitions regarding its history still exist. The sandhills, capped with the rustling, silky bents, looking down into the bay, are still there. The thrilling sea winds come and go, and the music of the shells on the beach is whispering as before, but the shrill wail of the curlew is never sounded from knoll to knoll now. The horn lantern is not seen by the roadsides, nor the quick flashlight that signalled the coast was clear; and the rattle of the horses' hoofs on the stones during the mystic night is never now heard. There is nothing to indicate, in fact, that this lonely, superb piece of England was once (not so long ago) a great centre of illicit trading. The smuggler and Revenue man have disappeared, and the scenes of their successes or failures, daring, comic, and sometimes tragic, are undisturbed save by nature's sights and sounds. Man-o'-war sailors (fine fellows though they be), with ribboned caps, and trousers that flap like sails of a ship tacking, have replaced the trim, gentlemanlike civilian of old. Some of the latter are still remembered with affection, and even veneration, by people who were young when the last of them passed away.

Smugglers of the Rock

Captain S—— was a man of enterprise, and never lost an opportunity of scheming to supplement the freight of the vessel he commanded. His common phrase was, "Look for business, and you'll meet it on the road." He was well known all over the Mediterranean, and had done much trade with the Spanish ports, so that he got to know a good deal about the character and methods of their business. On one occasion, at Gibraltar, a deputation of traders, as they called themselves, made him a proposition that was startling in its remunerative dimensions.

"I presume," said the captain, "this business which you are good enough to put before me is sound; there is no humbug about it?"

"Not one bit, captain. You undertake to do certain work for which we pay you before starting."

It was arranged that he should wire from his last port of call when passing down the Mediterranean. He fixed his mind on the amount he was to receive, and did not inquire too closely into the character of the business. He would have been virtuously indignant if any one had hinted that he was capable of going beyond the limits of stern rectitude, although he admitted the undertaking to be extraordinary, otherwise he would not have been so well paid for it. His knowledge of character told him that he was going to do business with a squad of rascals who knew no moral law, and yet the fascination of exciting enterprise held him in its grip. So it came to pass that he sent his telegram announcing approximately when he might be expected at Gibraltar, and asking them to have all in readiness against his arrival. In the early morning of the eighth day after leaving Malta, the steamer crept from under the Great Rock into the beautiful bay, and was promptly boarded by a few gentlemen of effusive manners who were greatly concerned about the health of Captain S——. The latter requested them to cease their chatter and to get to business.

"Are the craft ready?" said he.

"Oh yes," replied the Rock-scorpions; "but you will have to wait until dark before they can be brought from their moorings."

This was agreed to. The captain put his vessel alongside the coal hulk, and by noon the required bunker coal had been shipped, and through the kindness of the captain of the hulk she was allowed to remain alongside until darkness set in, on the plea of repairs being done to defective machinery. She was then slowly moved towards three feluccas which lay waiting in the bay. The night was still, and the moon shone bright and made the sea silvery by its reflection; but a large halo encircled it, and the seamen knew that foreboded stormy weather. "Telegraph boys" were coming up from the west very swiftly. There was to be trouble outside Cape Spartel, and they were anxious to get through the stream before the gale had developed strength. A boat came alongside. Two Levantines stepped aboard. The captain said—

"So you have come at last. Have you got the money with you? Let me have no wriggling, or I will have you put over the side and steam away without your merchandize."

"No, no, capitan, you must not do that! Come to the charthouse and you shall be paid at once."

After three-fourths of the agreed sum had been counted out the paymaster stuck, and said, "Capitan, you must be satisfied. We are poor men like yourself."

In an instant the captain was out of the charthouse *with his money*, and went on to the upper bridge and called out to his officers to see the gentlemen into their boat. They pleaded to him to come into the charthouse again, and every cent due to him would be handed over according to agreement.

"I did not mean what I said to be taken seriously," said the financial agent.

"But I did," replied the captain. "And take notice that if you wriggle again I will make short work of this business."

The balance of freight was handed over without further demur, and the craft taken in tow as arranged. It was urged that the heaviest laden of the three lighters should tow astern of the others. The engines were set easy ahead. The two scorpions were asked to get into their boat quickly. They wished the captain good luck, and gave him instructions to steer over to the African side of the gut, as the current was easier there. He was warned in true Levantine eloquence, and with an accent and tone that indicated anxiety for the success of the project, to look sharply after the "wolves" when they got off Tarifa, for this is the narrowest part of the entrance to the Mediterranean. It was clear that this traffic welcomed no publicity.

The C— — was soon plunging into a strong westerly swell, though there was as yet but little wind. They had got Tarifa abeam, when the look-out man reported a small vessel three points on the starboard bow. In a few more minutes the "wolves" announced themselves by a few small shot rattled against the smoke stack. Orders were given to the second officer to go aft with a hatchet, and when the signal was given he had to snap the tow-rope of the last felucca. All hands were ordered to lie low—*i.e.*, lie under shelter of the bulwarks. The captain and chief officer took shelter on the port side of the charthouse. The vessel's course was altered, but being so far over on the African coast there was not much room to play on. The firing was still directed at the funnel, though at times it was erratic. One of the seamen shouted, "I'm hit!" In an instant the captain blew his whistle, and the tow-line of No. 3 craft was cut. The steamer's speed increased, though it did not much matter so far as getting out of the fire zone was concerned, as the Spanish *Costaguardia's* attention became fixed on the abandoned craft.

"My God!" soliloquized the chief mate, "the Rock-scorpions are right. They have pounced upon the derelict like wolves. I almost wish I was there to see the effect when they realize they have been fooled, and they find that that craft is loaded with stones. It was just done in the nick of time; they might have compelled us to heave to."

"I would never have done that," said the captain. "I knew they would not risk being defeated in their object when they saw so excellent a prize thrown at them."

"They are setting the sail," observed the officer.

"Yes," responded the captain. "The gentlemen will find one of their craft anchored in Gibraltar Bay to-morrow morning, and may be the whole three. I do not like the look of it; both the wind and sea are making. I hope we may be able to reach to the westward of Trafalgar Bay before it gets worse."

Instructions were given to have the wounded seaman brought to the saloon, and it was found that he was not seriously injured. After the wound was dressed, orders were given to set the regular watch. Little progress was made during the night, owing to the heavy west wind. By six the following morning she was just a little west of Cape Spartel, and the wind had increased to a heavy gale. The engines had to be slowed down in order to save the two little vessels from being dragged under water; indeed, as it was, their hulls were sometimes buried. The captain saw that he was in for a tragedy if the craft were kept in tow. He did not like to slip them, as it meant certain capture, and while he was thinking out the wisest and best course to pursue, the problem was solved by the people aboard the feluccas letting go the tow-line, and the last that was seen of them was that they were heading towards the Spanish coast with small storm sails set.

Captain S——'s vessel had a severe passage, and on arrival in Falmouth he went to an hotel. In the course of the evening he was relating the incidents of the voyage, as was the custom with orthodox captains on arrival in port, and of course he included his experiences with the Rock-scorpions and their feluccas. Before he had completed the tale, the proprietor interposed by reading as follows from a shipping paper:—

> "Information was conveyed to the Spanish Customs Authority that a British steamer had run out of Gibraltar Bay with three feluccas laden with manufactured tobacco destined for Cadiz. She was to be intercepted at Tarifa by the coastguards, and the craft with their cargo were to have been seized. When she got to Tarifa the coastguards fired at her. The third lighter was slipped, boarded by the officials and their men, and taken behind the Rock, when it was discovered on removing the hatches that she was laden with stones. The other two parted their tow-ropes, and were driven through the Gut and captured. These were laden with tobacco. The stone-laden craft was obviously intended as a decoy, and but for the heavy gale that came on, the other two would have succeeded in reaching their destination."

A few months later, Captain S—— entered Gibraltar Bay, and was boarded by the chief commissioner of the last enterprise, accompanied by a friend, who was introduced as being engaged in "our" trade.

"Ah," said the former in genuine Rock-scorpion dialect, "The last was a great disaster; but it has never been said that you did not do all that was possible to carry out your contract properly. If there had been any appearance of not doing so, my friend and I would not have said that Captain S—— is the very man to carry out our new affair, which is doubly better than the other."

"Well, shut up about that," said the captain. "Come to the point. What is it you wish me to do?"

"Ah! capitan, but for the knowledge we have of your ability, and the affection my friends and myself have for you, we would have hesitated to show you this token of our much esteem."

"Shut up!" interjected the sailor. "I don't want a display of pretty nothings. I want business."

"Oh! capitan, why do you say such things when we are so anxious to put something your way. I tell you there are thousands of men that would be glad to have your chance. The job we have is this: three feluccas are lying up in the harbour laden with tobacco. Tonight you must lie off the town without anchoring, and they will be brought alongside. You must take the cargo aboard, and proceed off Amonti Pomoron. A pilot and interpreter will go with you, and you must not go near the land until darkness comes on, when craft showing signals which the pilot understands will be there to meet you and have men to tranship the cargo into lighters. You will have £400 for doing this—half in cash before leaving, and the other half on arrival at Amonti. The transaction will be quite straight."

"It seems to me so uncommonly like a huge smuggling affair, that I cannot entertain it," replied S——.

"No, no! my dear capitan; here you are mistaken. We would not ask such a thing of you. How can it be smuggling? The cargo is put aboard in neutral waters; you take it off the coast of Spain and deliver it as arranged. You get your money, and know nothing more about it. How can that be smuggling?"

"Well," said the captain, "it has nothing to do with me where the stuff comes from, or where it is going to. If you will give me five hundred pounds, all cash, before leaving here, I will agree to take it."

The Rock-scorpion gasped—

"What, five hundred pounds! Capitan, now do be reasonable. I tell you no other man would get the half of what you are offered."

"Very well, then," replied the captain, "it is off. Give it to the person who will do it for half."

"Certainly not; that is not what I mean," said the commissioner. "How can I face my friends with such news after all I have said to them about you? They will form a bad opinion of both you and myself."

"Oh! d—— both you and your friends. Get over the side, or I'll help you."

"Well, Capitan S——, I have never seen a man in such a temper before."

"Oh, go to——!"

"Oh no, no, capitan; don't say that. I cannot tell my friends of this."

"I wouldn't take your stuff for a thousand pounds now," said the captain.

"Forgive me, my best friend. I did not mean to be offensive; you have misunderstood my meaning. I will give you five hundred pounds, though I know I will have to pay one hundred out of my own purse. It is very hard."

The captain hesitated, but was overcome by the thought of making so large a clean profit without involving any material loss of time. In less than an hour after darkness came on the cargo was being put aboard with amazing facility. The first lighter was nearly discharged, when the captain asked the agent to pay the freight. This gentleman, with many greasy apologies, informed him that he had only half of the money with him. He could not get his friends to agree to pay all before starting, "but they will agree to pay half here and the other half as soon as the lighters come to you at Amonti." "Very well, then; I won't take another bale in, and will steam away at once."

"But," said the cunning Rock-scorpion, "you have a lighter of goods aboard. You are very dreadful for talking about running away with it."

"You make me sick," said the captain, with a killing look of scorn.

"Capitan, you say queer things to your best friends. Now, I tell you what I will do: I will on my own responsibility give you in cash two-thirds now, and the other third I pledge myself will be paid at Amonti. It would be a scandal to all concerned to allow it to drop at the present time."

"Scandal be d——d!" replied the commander. "You're a fine lot to talk about scandal—you who would rob Jesus Christ of his shoe-strings."

"Capitan, you do me wrong; I would never do the things you say."

"Stump up the dross like a man, then, and don't stand whining there like a sucking turkey craving for pity," retorted Captain S——. A look of injured piety came over the old rascal's face, who was playing a game of Levantine jugglery, subtle and crafty.

"Ah," said he, "I am so sorry. Indeed, I cannot express my grief that you should have changed in so short a time from the kind, generous capitan of old times long ago to the very cruel, disobliging person of this minute, who calls me names and refuses to reciprocate kindness for kindness. I think my friends will say that I tell lies, which they would not think of me, when I tell them that you have become morose and disobliging. They will stare and say that my judgment has been deceived. But to show my trust in you, nevertheless, I will, as I have said, give you two-thirds cash, and the other third you will be paid at your destination. No other man in Gibraltar would do the same; but we are old friends who have done business together before—not profitable, but still it was business, very hard business. Come, now, capitan, do be reasonable, and do not look at me as though you would like to strike my face with your fist."

The captain had been standing in a reflective mood during the Rock-scorpion's harangue, obviously reviewing the whole position and the policy that should be adopted. He was dubious as to the wisdom of accepting the terms offered; but seeing that the risk to him was less than it was to them, he spontaneously replied—

"Agreed! But I warn *you*, and you must intimate the warning to your friends, if there is any attempt at deceiving me, or any reluctance shown at the other end to pay the balance of freight, I will steam off with the merchandise and the men you propose sending with me, and I don't care to say what will become of them."

"Shake hands," said the wily agent; "and I give you my word of honour, which everybody trusts but you since you came this time, that there will be no trouble made. Now come to the charthouse and take over the cash."

This formality was speedily accomplished, though not without a further attempt to reduce the cash payment on the plea that it would endanger his professional reputation in the eyes of his commercial friends.

"I care nothing for your reputation," murmured the candid sailor. "What I want is two-thirds freight, so stump it all up, or I will have it taken from you and then hoist you into your boat."

Whereupon the agent became afflicted with grief at his dear friend's threatened cruelty.

"Really, my best friend, I must not give way here, but I will shed tears when I get to my silent home, and speak with myself of the change that has come to your mind."

"Don't you bother about shedding tears; you see that your friends play the game," said the inexorable captain. "I will carry out my part; but, by heavens! if your people don't carry out theirs, you shall all pay dearly for it."

"You are too excited on this occasion, my dear capitan, and for this I am sorry, as I like to see you as usual. I tell you if they do not play the fair way, I will be responsible and be very vexed."

"Shut up, you blatherskite; the cargo is all aboard. Get into your boat quick, and remember what I have said to you when you can overcome the effects of your wriggling and dodging. Your cargo can only be delivered on one condition. Keep in mind what it is. Begone, and never let me see your evil countenance again."

Thus spoke the enterprising commander, who had begun to realize that he was having dealings with a gang whom he would have to fight in order to get his own. The engines were put at full speed, and kept at that until she was fifty miles north-west of Cape Spartel, when they were slowed so that she might not arrive before the appointed time. As the vessel trailed sinuously over the quiet sea, the captain's thoughts were centred on material things and the reception he was likely to have on meeting the men his mind's eye pictured as cut-throat ruffians. He had several conferences with the interpreter, whose look and speech he regarded as a revelation of villainy. He was tall and slim, with ricketty legs, dark shifty eyes, a low receding forehead, and a mouth and chin that indicated the animal. The captain felt instinctively the approach of trouble, and frankly told the wretch, who he knew was deceiving him, that every bale of tobacco would be held until after the freight was paid over in gold sovereigns; and with an air of ostentatious authority he gave instructions to have all the muskets and revolvers loaded and ready in case they should be required. The hideous scoundrel fixed his eye on the captain, and with ironic accent intimated he could not help being filled with concern when he heard the orders given to prepare the firearms.

"Capitan, we are not pirates; we are respectable men carrying on a respectable trade. You need not prepare anything; we are honest tradesmen."

The captain laughed heartily at this comic assurance of fidelity, and felt convinced that a deep impression had been made, as the interpreter shortly after was seen vigorously conversing with his two compatriots. The one had been introduced as the representative of the owner of the cargo, and the other the pilot, whose business it was to direct the captain to that part of the coast where the craft was awaiting the vessel's arrival. The treacherous dusk was casting its shadows over them, and had brought with it a weird sound of the moaning wind. The crew stood in little knots, talking earnestly to each other. Obviously they conversed of the night's work, and all the grave possibilities that lay in front of them. For the most part they wore an anxious look on their faces, but there was one there whose eye was full of sparkling fun, and whose face beamed with a self-satisfied expectation of exhilarating dangers. The captain called him to the bridge, and gave him some specific orders as to how he was to act when certain signals were given. The chaste and simple motto of "the blow first and jaw afterwards" guided him, and he was only profane when discipline demanded it. His superstitious tendencies were in an ordinary way an anxiety to him, but on the night in question the only signs he gave of being affected in this way was by the half coherent remark to the captain that he did not like to hear the shrill wail of the wind through the rigging; "it seems to be speaking to us of some trouble near at hand." Suddenly the interpreter called out, "I see the feluccas." In a moment all thought of the wail of the wind had disappeared, and this fine athletic seaman was commanding his men like a hero. He had been told by his captain that there would more than likely be rough work to do, and he prepared for it with a skill and vigour that left no doubt as to how his instructions would be carried out. "Give the signal at the proper time," said he, "and leave the rest to me." A shipwrecked crew was being taken home in the steamer, and these, together with her own crew, made the number look formidable, and although they were never requested to give assistance, they offered it in case of need. Undoubtedly the addition to the ordinary crew had a moral effect upon the Spaniards.

The craft came alongside, and her crew jumped aboard and commenced to handle the bales. They were peremptorily stopped by the captain giving instructions that not a single bale was to be allowed to pass into the lighters until the freight was paid and he had given orders. Soon there was a carnival of foes. The captain called to the interpreter to bring the man with the money to the saloon. The interpreter came but not the man. The former said the money was coming on the second lighter, but the one alongside must be loaded and sent away first.

"No, no!" interposed the captain; "no money, no bales." He would wait until the second lighter came, which could easily be placed alongside astern of the first one. In a short time number two came, and was moored as directed. A large number of men jumped aboard from both craft. The captain again called out to bring the man with the money, and again no one turned up but the interpreter. This time he was defiant. He put his back against the saloon side, folded his arms and began—

"Capitan, you see the number of people aboard your vessel. They can take her from you, if they so wish it. I tell you frankly we have no money; but, by God! we must and shall have the tobacco."

The captain had been reared amidst a race of men who had imbued him with the importance of hitting decisively and with promptness, when confronted with situations which demanded physical action. In an instant he had hold of the scoundrel, who, he was convinced now, was the leader of a plot to take the cargo by force. Under peremptory compulsion, the Levantine was rushed on deck, informed that he had miscalculated with whom he had to deal, and that any one who attempted to carry out his threat would be fired upon.

"I give you fair warning there shall be no half measures, and I command you to inform your friends what I have said; and also state to them that as soon as I have been paid my freight, they will not only be allowed to have the cargo, but I will instruct my crew to assist in the transhipment."

It never will be known now what this plant of grace intimated precisely to his colleagues, but the general impression was at the time that the captain's message had not been conveyed verbatim. Soon the babble of tongues charged the air and gave an impression of Bedlam. The captain had resolved upon a course of action which was strenuous. He had given certain orders to the chief engineer, and was standing on the lower bridge reviewing the situation, when the second officer came up to him and said in a whisper—

"The Spaniards are all armed to the teeth, sir."

"All right," said the captain, "they will soon be disarmed. Meanwhile, as a precaution, put our men on their guard. This business must be carried through vigorously, and with dash."

At this juncture the interpreter, apparently with the intention of breaking the deadlock, attempted to come on the bridge, and was warned if he put his foot on the ladder he (the captain) would jump on top of him. He did so, and the next moment he was flattened on the deck. The Spaniards, in great excitement, surrounded the two. At last, one of the shipwrecked men spoke to them in Spanish, and the master asked him if he could really speak Spanish. He replied in the affirmative.

"Then," said the captain, "translate to these men that I do not wish to hold the cargo, but that my agreement was for the freight to be paid immediately the craft came alongside."

This pronouncement seemed to make an impression, but they still coveted and cavilled for the goods. They endeavoured to persuade the master of the steamer, who had gone on to the bridge again, to anchor, and the money would be brought off in the morning. He prevaricated with them, and at the same time told the chief engineer secretly to put the engines easy ahead. She was brought head on to the sea, and the wind having risen, a nasty swell came with it, which caused the lighters to jump and put jerky strains on their moorings. A few of their crew jumped aboard, and were trying to pass additional ropes around the rigging of the steamer when the captain blew his whistle. In an instant the tow-rope of the forward lighter was cut; then it was that the Spaniards realized what was happening. They remonstrated with the captain; they shouted to each other excitedly; those that had not got aboard the feluccas flew along the deck and jumped, one after the other, on to their vessel as she swung round. Another shrill whistle, and the last rope of lighter No. 2 was snapped. Captain S—— called out to the interpreter, who was pleading piteously to allow them to have only some of the cargo, to jump at once if he did not wish to lose his passage, and to be taken away with the steamer. He quickly realized his true position, and sprang over the stern. It was supposed that he was picked up by one of the craft. They then commenced to fire wildly from the feluccas, but little harm was done, and in a brief time the steamer had travelled far outside the range of their guns, and was heading towards Cape St. Vincent, with the whole of the contraband aboard of a value of something like £5000. The question of how it was to be disposed of was a problem not easily solved. The first thought was to take it to Lisbon. This idea having broken down, the next thought was one of the Channel Islands (Jersey or Guernsey). This also, for specific reasons, gave way. It was then decided to take it to the port of discharge of the ordinary cargo; but after calculating all the trouble, the payment of duty, time lost, and possible legal technicalities, the captain resolved that the best and cleanest way of disposing of it was to jettison the whole of it. This decision brought him into sharp conflict with his chief officer, who entirely disagreed with such a course.

"Is it for this," he said, "that we risked being shot and having the steamer seized and confiscated? The tobacco belongs to us by right of conquest, as well as by moral right, and it will be an abomination to throw it overboard. Even if we make only a thousand pounds out of it, it is always something; but to put it into the sea would be sinful beyond description. I cannot bring myself to be a party to such a thing."

The decision of the captain was irrevocable, in spite of the persuasive eloquence of a deputation of the crew and engineers. So, after passing the Burlings, orders were given to cut the bales, save the packing, and shovel the tobacco overboard. This very nearly caused open revolt, but the captain made a few tactful statements which had good effect. He presented a case that could not be controverted, and they yielded to the inevitable. The jettisoning commenced with bad grace, and a continual growl was kept up until the captain himself was overcome by the sight of the beautiful tobacco being thrown away. He called a halt, after persuading himself that a new idea might be presented to the mind as time went on, which would show how a profit could be made without risking any vital interest; but this only endured for a couple of days. No really sound idea came, and so the work of destruction was resumed until only half a dozen bales were left, and it was resolved to hold these whatever happened. The mate was a sailor of the old school, and clung to the grog and tobacco traditions of the eighteenth century. He might have forgiven the purveyors of defective food, but if bad grog and tobacco were supplied there was no forgiveness for that, here or hereafter! He believed in the crew being served with grog whenever they were called upon to do extra work, such as shortening sail or setting it, and although he never allowed smoking when on duty, or expectoration on the quarter-deck, a skilful seaman was all the more popular with him if he chewed. His opinion was that they did better work, and more of it, when they rolled a quid about in their mouths. If his attention was called to a small boy who was practising the habit, a pride-of-race smile would come into his face, and his laughing eyes indicated the joy it was giving him. Then he would say, "Thank God, the race is not becoming extinct. I have always hope of a youngster turning out satisfactorily if he works well and chews well." As a matter of fact, his conviction was that a boy or man who adopted the practice did so instinctively because they were born sailors, and were true types of British manhood. Indeed, he regarded manhood as strictly confined to his own class, though on many occasions I have seen volcanic evidences of shattered faith. It was not so much the money value of the tobacco, but the *racial affection he had for it* that caused him to feel indignant at the suggestion of it being thrown to the waves.

The second day subsequent to this conflict, it was the first mate's afternoon watch below. He had partaken of his midday meal, and went to the bridge to have a smoke. As he looked down at the bales of goods, he said to the second mate—

"However the thought of destroying that beautiful stuff can have entered the mind of man I cannot fathom. I think I have got him persuaded to leave well alone. It must be nothing short of stark lunacy."

And the two men were agreed that had their captain *been as short of it as they* had been one time and another he would not talk such foolishness. The chief mate intimated that he was going to have a nap, but that his mind was torn with presentiment which he could not speak about calmly. At four o'clock when he came on deck he was made aware of what had taken place during his watch below, whereupon he lapsed into a kind of inarticulate stupor, and could not speak the unutterable. He placed his right hand on his brow, and then on his left breast, and stood gazing at the long Atlantic rollers, which had the appearance of an uneven reef of rocks. The stage of stupor and grief was superseded by that of resigned indignation. He plaintively called out—

"Well, I'll—be—teetotally—d——d! Miles of sea to be paved with that beautiful tobacco! Retribution will come to somebody; and, by thunder! it should come with a clattering vengeance. I will never forget the sight as long as I have breath."

The captain came up to him, and seeing that his mind was centred on what he regarded as not only a calamity but a crime, he was so much amused at his ludicrously pathetic appearance that he laughingly repeated—

"Oh, for the touch of a vanished hand, and the sound of a voice that is still."

The inappropriate words were merely used as a piece of chaff, but Mr. S—— was not in a chaffing mood, so he retorted that he did not see where the humour came in, and there was nothing to laugh at, and so on. He then walked on to the bridge, and he and the captain were not on friendly speaking terms any more during the voyage.

At midnight on the sixth day after parting company from the Spaniards, the vessel was hove to to take a pilot aboard. Captain S—— took him aside as soon as he boarded, and asked him in an undertone if he ever did anything in the contraband line. He held up his hands as though he were horrified at the suggestion, and exclaimed—

"Not for the world, captain!"

"Very well," replied the captain; "you go below, and I will join you in a minute or two, after giving orders to the steward to make tea for us."

As a matter of fact, he remained behind to give orders to the mate to throw overboard the remaining six bales, which was a further trial to the grief-stricken officer; and having done this the captain joined the pilot, and entered into conversation with him. The two men were not long in discovering that they each belonged to the brotherhood of Freemasons. This put them on easy terms at once, and encouraged the pilot to inquire into the meaning of the words spoken to him on boarding.

"I do not quite know how I stand in relation to that," said the captain. "Indeed, I am perplexed as to the plan I ought to adopt. So many difficulties confront me as the scheme of development goes on; but so far as I have been able to work out the problem, I think my attitude must be straightforward, and that I should make a full voluntary statement to the authorities. Meanwhile, if you pledge me your Masonic honour to keep it a secret until I have made it public, I will tell you the whole story."

The undertaking was readily given, and long before the whole story was told, the pilot's Christian virtues had broken down. At frequent intervals while the narrative was being told he interjected, "Oh! why didn't you tell me?" His mind was transfixed. Then the processes of it became confused. The vision of wealth and the reckless squandering of some of it took possession of him, and with uncontrolled zeal he called out—

"My God! what a story! O captain, why didn't you tell me what it was at once, and not waste time? Let us get to work without delay. I will undertake to land what you have got on an island and share the proceeds with you."

"Too late, too late, my friend. You have thrown away an opportunity which may never come to you again," replied the master, with a mischievous twinkle in his eye. "Transactions of this kind are done spontaneously and with vigour—they are not to be dreamed about."

"I admit my error, captain; but, oh! how was I to know? Surely you do not mean to tell me that the balance of the tobacco has been thrown overboard since I came here?"

"Yes, it is all gone. We do not hesitate when we face the inevitable, no matter what the sacrifice may be."

"Well, I'm blowed!" soliloquized the pilot. "It will take me some time to get over this little bit of history."

"I daresay," said the captain; "but it is time you took charge—she is now within your jurisdiction. What do you say to going on the bridge? You will find the chief officer there, with whom you may condole, if it be safe for a stranger to speak of so delicate a subject to him. You will, perhaps, find him stupefied with grief and shame at the unpatriotic conduct of his commander, and I daresay his language will impress you with the venerable traditions cherished by his class when things are supposed to have gone wrong."

The pilot greeted the chief officer cordially, but did not receive a very polite response to his attempts to draw him into conversation about his recent experiences, and was cut short in a sailorly fashion by being told if he wanted any information about experiences, as he called them, to go and ask "that — — fool of a skipper about it."

"I have had a little conversation with him," replied the pilot; "and it does seem to me extraordinary—and if I were not here I might almost say an outrage—that no other course could be found than utter sacrifice."

"Oh, don't talk to me!" exclaimed the vivacious mate, in a flood of passion. "You call it extraordinary and an outrage! Is that a proper name for such wickedness? You ask me what I think of it? I tell you I cannot think. You talk about outrage! I say, sir, it is joining outrage to injustice, and I cannot believe that any other than a frozen-souled fool would have done it. There is not a glimmering of common-sense in it. The wonder is that he didn't take it back to the scoundrels, for pity's sake!"

This outburst of withering scorn encouraged the pilot to ask what the sailors thought of it.

"Go and ask them, if you want to hear something you've never heard before."

The captain, who was in the charthouse, could not help hearing these interesting opinions of himself, nor could he help enjoying the rugged humour of them. His mate had his peculiarities, but he never doubted his loyalty to himself, and he was sure that on reflection he would come to see the wisdom of disentanglement. He went on to the bridge as though all was serene, asked a few questions of the pilot, and settled down until the vessel arrived at her discharging port.

On landing, a message-boy told him there was a telegram at the office for him. He eagerly asked if he knew where it was from. The boy replied, "Gibraltar." He requested the messenger to get it for him, and found it was from the agent who shipped the tobacco, the purport of it being to offer him £500 to bring it back, and intimating that a letter was on the way. When this came to hand, it explained exhaustively the reason the freight was not paid as agreed, and boldly accused the port authorities and officials of having organized a plot in order to accomplish their own evil ends. This precious document was signed by the writer, and, needless to say, was not replied to. As a necessary protection to himself, the master had a declaration signed by the whole of the crew, stating that they had no tobacco concealed or in their possession other than that shown to the Custom-house officers.

As is usual after a vessel arrives in a home port, and is properly moored and decks cleared up, the crew go aft, draw a portion of their wages, and then go ashore. They had a fine tale to relate, and it may be taken for granted that no incident connected therewith lost any of its flavour in the process of narration. It would appear that the sailors got drunk and "peached" in a most grotesque way. They declared that although much of the contraband had been disposed of, this was only done as a blind, and that there were tons beneath the iron ore and in the peaks and bunkers, and all over the vessel. The story spread, and grew as it was passed along, until it became the most colossal smuggling enterprise ever known in the country. The captain came on board at noon on the day following the arrival, and found a large number of Custom-house officers on board. Some were in the holds digging vigorously at the ore with picks and shovels. Their coats were off, and their shirt sleeves doubled up. Others were on deck ready for action, but the chief mate prevented them going into the forepeak, which caused both suspicion and irritation. The captain gave them permission. Two went forth full of hope and confidence that they were on the point of reaping their reward. They had no sooner got down than indescribable cries for God to help them were heard. A rush was made to see what had happened. The lights were out, and nothing was visible. They groped their way to the peak ladder, and were nearly dead with fright when they reached the deck. When they had sufficiently recovered, they said that there was something in the peak alive, which kept butting up against them. They were sure it wasn't a man, and that it must be something evil. An Irish sailor stood close by laughing and jeering at them, and in genuine brogue he charged them with being haunted by their own "evil deeds."

"You had no business there," said he, "and to prove to you that I am right I'll swear divil a thing is there in the peak but cargo gear and other stores. I'll go down myself and face the evil one you talk about."

And down he went, but the fright of the officers was feeble to the Irishman's. He shrieked and flew on deck shouting, "Be God, you're right, he's there!"

The chief mate suspected what it was, but was not keen on going down himself or ordering any one else to do so, so the anchor light was lowered down and shone upon the captain's pet goat. It had been long aboard for the purpose of supplying milk to the captain and his wife. The peak hatch had been off, and Nannie, accustomed to go wherever she pleased, strayed into the darkness and tumbled down. The incident stopped all work for a time, and created a lot of good-humoured chaff. The Irishman was especially droll, and endeavoured to carry it off by swearing he knew it was the goat, but he wanted some other fellow to have a go at it. "But no fear," said he; "every one of them was dying with funk."

After a time the captain thought it right to disillusion the officer in ⁓e, and going up to him asked the meaning of the raid.

" replied the officer, "we have information that there is a large ⁓co aboard, and that some of it is in the forepeak, but most ⁓ of feet below the iron ore."

⁓e had a lot of it a few days since, but there is not ⁓ow of. Every particle has been thrown overboard. this point."

"But," said the officer, "what about the packing? My men have come across a large quantity."

"That is very true," said the commander; "the packing is the only thing we saved. Now get your men ashore, there's a good fellow. You are only working them to death for no earthly reason."

"But the sailors say the tobacco was emptied out of the packing and covered over with ore."

"Well, if you believe the sailors and you don't believe me, go on digging. I can only repeat, the search is futile."

"Very well," replied the disconcerted official, "I shall withdraw all my men but two, who must remain to watch and make sure of there being no concealment. Not that I disbelieve you. It is merely a formal precaution which I hope you will think nothing of."

The whole affair had been reported to the Collector of Customs, and the master was informed that all things considered, the best thing had been done in ridding himself of an awkward encumbrance. In a few days an emissary of the Gibraltar syndicate had an interview with the captain, and then disappeared. It was said that he was strongly advised to disappear, lest he should be detained by legal authority.

The owner received the freight paid in advance with obvious pleasure, like a good, Christian gentleman; but the intelligence of how it was earned and the disastrous conclusion of the undertaking was listened to with studied gravity. A sermon on the danger of little sins such as covetousness and the growing love of money was impressively preached. The owner was convinced that if ever the gentlemen involved in this little transaction got the opportunity they would take the master's life, so in the goodness of his heart he determined that the vessel should not call there for coal until the spirit of vengeance had had ample time to cool down.

More than twelve months had elapsed since these affairs occurred, when the owner was offered a charter from the Black Sea, but one of the unalterable conditions was that the vessel should call at Gibraltar for orders. The captain strongly urged his owner not to lose so good a charter because of his anxiety for him, but he was obdurate until the captain said —

"Then I shall have to resign my command. I cannot go on like this longer."

"If you make this the alternative, then I must give way; but the responsibility is yours alone," was the reply.

The charter was signed, and on a fine summer day two months after, the C— — let go her anchor in Gibraltar Harbour to await her orders. A tall, fine-looking man came aboard to solicit business of a legitimate character. He spoke English with fluency and an almost correct accent. The captain knew he had some business connection with the syndicate, but did not give him any reason to suppose he had this knowledge. He was cognisant of the characteristics of these people, and determined that his safety was in assuming an injured attitude, and making a slashing attack on the blackguards who had done him so much harm. Excepting for a slight humorous twist in the corner of his mouth, Mr. ---- received the onslaught with perfect equanimity. The captain asked if he knew the rascal P— —.

"Yes," said he, "I know him. He is a bad lot, and I advise you never to trust him again. But if you wish me to, I will convey to him what you say; and I think you would be perfectly justified in carrying out your intention." (The intention was to horsewhip him publicly.)

The following morning the captain landed with his wife and family, and boldly walked past the resorts of the men who he had reason to believe were on his track. He kept his hand on the revolver which was in his trouser-pocket, and the sound of every foot behind him seemed to be a message of warning. This ordeal went on for four days, and never a sign of the dreaded assassins was seen. On the afternoon of the fifth day he was walking down towards the boat-landing to go on board, when his eye came in contact with the interpreter and the whole gang that were concerned in the tobacco enterprise. There was a look of murder on their villainous faces, which the captain said would haunt him to his dying day. He spontaneously and without thought said to his wife, who walked beside him—

"I see the smugglers. Don't look!"

But it came so suddenly upon her that she could not restrain the temptation of seeing them, and the impression of their malignant looks had a lasting effect on her. When they reached the boat, the gentleman who had boarded her on arrival was there. He drew the captain aside, and whispered that he was being shadowed, and urged that a double watch be kept at the entrance to the cabin. As a matter of policy the captain assumed an air of defiance. He promised a sanguinary reception for them if they attempted to come near his vessel, and he believes to this day that this alone was the means of preventing an attack.

Next morning orders were brought off, and no time was lost in weighing anchor and clearing out, and he has never visited the place since.

A Pasha before Plevna

The Eastern Question was ablaze. Mr. Gladstone had published his "bag and baggage" pamphlet, and made his Blackheath speech in September 1876. Both are memorable for the strong feelings they generated for and against the object of his attack. Benjamin Disraeli had become the Earl of Beaconsfield, and had made his bellicose and Judaical speech at the Lord Mayor's Banquet. The fleet had been ordered to Besika Bay, and the metropolitan Press was busy backing Turkish saintliness for all it was worth. The Black Sea ports were crowded with steamers, and a great rush was made to get them loaded before hostilities broke out. In a few days there were but two vessels left in — — Harbour. The last cart-loads of grain in bags were being shipped. The vessel was held by a slip-rope at bow and stern, and as soon as she was loaded they let go, and the pilot took her to the outer harbour and anchored. The captain went to the town to clear his ship and sign bills of lading, and great exertions were made by his agents and himself to have this smartly done so that he could sail before darkness set in. After his business was done, he came to the landing and was about to get into his boat when a gentleman stepped up to him, and in an undertone said—

"Come to my office; I have something important to communicate to you. Don't, for God's sake, open your lips here. The very stones feel as if they were spying at me."

The captain hesitated, but his friend whispered—

"You must come; it is urgent, and it will be made worth your while."

Whereupon the cautious commander fell like a slaughtered lamb. They were soon alone within the four walls of a sumptuously-furnished private office.

"What's the game?" asked the impatient captain, uneasily.

"This is it," said his friend, coming close up to him and speaking in a low voice: "I have a secret job for you."

"Is there danger attached to it?" asked the captain.

"Yes, a good deal," replied his friend; "and I have chosen you to do it, because I know you will carry it out successfully if you'll take the risk."

"That's all very well," responded the captain, "but I don't care to overburden myself with danger and risk of confiscation, without I'm handsomely recompensed for it."

"Hush!" said his friend, nervously; "I think I hear voices. If we are overheard by any one, we may be betrayed and pounced upon at any moment."

After listening, he was reassured, and intimated that the worthy skipper would be well rewarded.

"That entirely alters the question," said the captain. "How much am I to have, and what is it you wish me to do?"

"You are to have two hundred and fifty pounds if you succeed in getting a distinguished Turkish pasha and his suite from here, and land them at Scutari."

"What!" exclaimed the commander. "Do you expect me to run the gauntlet with a Turkish pasha for two hundred and fifty pounds? Why, his head is worth thousands, to say nothing about the danger I run of having my ship confiscated, and myself sent to Siberia. Do not let us waste time. I will risk it for a thousand pounds, and put my state-room at his disposal."

The agent demurred, but the captain was for some time obdurate. However, seven hundred and fifty for the owners with two hundred for the captain was, after keen negotiation, agreed upon. It was further arranged that the steamer was not to sail until after midnight, so that the risk of stoppage would be lessened, and in rowing off as soon as it came dark, the oars were to be muffled.

"Leave these matters to me," said the captain. "How many passengers are there?"

"Six," said the agent. "They are in hiding. I will undertake to bring them aboard, with their baggage, in good time. Extreme care must be used in getting them away, as we may be watched. I have had to use 'palm oil' liberally, but even that may not prevent their betrayal and arrest."

"Well, then," said the shrewd commander, "under these circumstances I must have my freight before the risk actually begins."

It took some time for the agent to make up his mind to part with the money in advance, but the captain intimated that unless it was paid at once he would throw the business up. This promptly settled the matter, and a pledge was given by the enterprising captain to relax no effort or dash—"Combined with caution," said the agent—to fulfil his important mission. At 10 p.m., he was rowed alongside the steamer without having been interrupted or spoken to from the guardship or the sentries at the forts. After the gig was hoisted to the davits, the chief officer and chief engineer were asked to go to the saloon, where specific instructions were given as to the mode of procedure. The anchor was to be hove short at once very quietly. All lights had to be put out or blinded, and a full head of steam up at the hour of sailing. The officers were made aware of the job that had been undertaken, and relished the excitement of it. At 11.30 the passengers, with a large amount of baggage, came alongside and were taken aboard; and as a double precaution, the distinguished pasha and his attendants went down the forepeak until the vessel got outside. Their goods were put into the upper side-bunkers, and a wooden bulkhead put up to obscure them from view in case the vessel was boarded before getting clear. At midnight the anchor was weighed, and the steamer slipped out into the Black Sea. Every ounce of steam was used to make speed, and she was soon into safety so far as distance could help her.

The passengers, composed of the pasha, his priest, cook, interpreter, and servant, were then brought from their hiding-place and taken to the captain's private room. The vessel by this time was enveloped in a dense black fog. The first blast of the steam whistle startled the party, and the panic-stricken interpreter rushed on to the bridge. In a confusion of languages he implored the captain to say whether there was danger, and begged him to come to his master and his priest and reassure them that the whistle was being blown to let passing vessels know of their whereabouts and the course they were steering.

"Ah," said he, "my master is a brave, clever soldier; but like most soldiers, he does not know anything about the sea, and was in consequence uneasy when he heard the shrill sound of the whistle. Indeed, it made him change colour; he thought it might be a Russian privateer demanding you to stop. And the priest did not wait one minute; he went on to his knees and bowed his head in prayer, and the pasha ordered me to come to you quick. You must not think that I was nervous, captain; I was very excited only."

"Very well," replied the captain, smiling. "You may call it excitement, but I should call it white funk, the way you conducted yourself on my bridge. Why, you spoke every language in the universe!"

"Ah, that was not funk, captain; that was what you call confusion, caused by anxiety for that brave soldier in your cabin, and his spiritual adviser.

Besides, captain, how can you speak to one of your own countrymen in this fashion, and accuse him of talking so many tongues! I am a Maltese, and have interpreted for many years for my good friend, Osman Pasha."

"What!" cried the captain. "Is this the Turkish patriot, Osman Pasha?"

"Now, captain, *you* are excited; but I do not say that you speak many languages. Keep cool, and I will tell you. It is not Osman, but it is very near him, being his lieutenant or aide-de-camp."

"Is it Suleiman?"

"No, it is not."

"Then who the devil is it? By Jupiter! I believe it *is* Osman."

"I dare not tell you his name; he has been reconnoitring, and has had narrow escapes."

"That's not what I want to know. Tell me straight away—is it Osman Pasha, or is it not?"

"Captain," said the wily interpreter, "this is a secret mission. I cannot tell secrets that may get us all into trouble; but I will inform you that you will hear of this warrior during the next few months. I must ask you to come and see him. He cannot speak one word of English. Bring your chart, as he is sure to ask you to point out to him exactly our position."

The captain followed the interpreter into the presence of a majestic-looking person, who saluted him with kindly dignity. His face wore a thoughtful appearance; his eyes were penetrating, and under a massive forehead there rested well-developed eyebrows, betokening keen observation. His chin and nose were strong, and altogether his general looks, if not handsome, were comely. He gave the commander a real, big-hearted grip of the hand, which settled the question of friendship for him at once. Sailors detest a "grisly shake of the flipper." Likes and dislikes are invariably fixed by this test. The pasha was exceedingly cordial; asked, through his interpreter, all sorts of questions about the British Government, British statesmen, admirals, and generals, and the Army and Navy; but, above all, he was anxious to hear whether the British people were for or against Turkey. He was aware that Disraeli was with his nation, and regretted the attitude of Gladstone. He said poor Turkey had many enemies, and when the captain told him that he thought the bulk of the British people were in favour of Disraeli's policy, he held out his hand again in token of appreciation. The captain spoke very frankly about the Bulgarian atrocities, and the bad policy of the Turkish Government with her subject races. The pasha admitted that reforms ought to be given, but held that the Balkan insurrections were encouraged by Russia in order to ultimately get hold of Constantinople.

"My Government," said he, "is a better Government than that of Russia. We do not treat our people worse than she does hers. Are there no atrocities committed in Russia proper, in Siberia, in Poland? Why does Mr. Gladstone not demand that Russia shall give reforms to her subject races? Is it because she is big, and near to India, and calls herself a Christian nation? We are Mohammedans; and our religion teaches honesty, cleanness, sobriety, devotion to our God and his prophet Mahomet, and we adhere to it. Does the Russian adhere to his religion, which I admit, if carried out, is as good as ours? I think our consistency is superior to theirs, and the extent of our cruelty no worse, though I do not justify it. But do you think that the Servians, Armenians, Herzegovinians, Montenegrins, and Bulgarians are saints? Do you think that the Turkish people and Governors have not been provoked to retaliation? There may have been excesses, but no one who knows the different races will say that the Turks are all bad, or that the subject races are all good."

He then requested to be shown the position of the steamer on the chart, asked if there was any danger of collision if the fog continued, and hoped she was steaming full speed, as he must get to Constantinople without delay. The captain informed him that so long as he heard the whistle going the fog was still on, and it might become necessary to ease down as she drew towards the regular track of vessels; and when the danger of collision was explained to him, he agreed that it was necessary to guard against it, but asked through his interpreter that he should be shown the chart every four hours, which was agreed. The interpreter then intimated that the priest would hold a service previous to retiring to rest, and during the passage they would be held before and after every meal. The food, cooking utensils, and cook were provided by themselves. They would not eat the food of Christians, or use their utensils for the purpose of preparing it. In fact, what with the weird, shrill wail of their "yahing" prayers, the intolerable smell of their cooking, the smoke from their "hubblebubbles," and a perpetual run of messages coming from the pasha (while he was awake) to the officer in charge, they became somewhat of a nuisance before the first twenty-four hours had expired. The officers could not get their proper rest, which caused them to feel justified in becoming profane, and wishing the Turkish windpipes would snap.

The fog lifted, as it generally does, a little before noon, on the day after sailing, and an accurate latitude was got; but during the afternoon it shut down blacker than ever. The engines had to be slowed, and the whistle was constantly going. The pasha's anxiety to get to his destination was giving him constant worry, and he became more and more troublesome. The interpreter explained that the Sultan was waiting to consult his master about the plan of campaign, and other military matters, and that the delay was making the pasha impatient; but in spite of annoying pressure, the captain refused to depart from the wise precaution of going slow while the fog lasted. At midnight it cleared up a little, and the engines were put at full speed until 8 a.m. the following morning, when they ran into a bank of fog again. The speed was slackened to dead slow, and as she was nearing the Bosphorus land the lead was kept going; but, owing to the great depth of water, sounding is little guide towards keeping vessels clear of the rocks of that steep and iron-bound coast. Currents run with rapid irregularity, and in no part of the world is navigation more treacherous than there. According to the reckoning, the vessel was within four miles of the entrance to the Bosphorus, but no prudent navigator would have risked going farther until he could see his way; so orders were given to stop her. This brought more urgent messages from the pasha. As the day wore on and the mist still continued, all hope of getting into the Bosphorus had disappeared. The pasha sent for the captain, and said he must be at Constantinople that evening.

"Well," said the captain to the interpreter, "tell your master that if the Sultan and all his concubines were to ask me to go ahead I would have to refuse."

Then he proceeded to point out the dangers on the chart. This did not appeal to the pasha's military understanding. What he wanted was to be landed somewhere, and he did not regard running the vessel ashore with any disastrous consequences to himself until he was assured that the rocks were so steep that even in a calm the vessel might sink in deep water and everybody be drowned.

"Anyhow," said the captain, "I'm not going to try it on; so you must inform your master of my definite decision. He cannot be more anxious than I am. I've scarcely closed my eyes since we left, and if this continues I must face another night of it."

He then went on to the bridge, and had only been there about half an hour when his persistent passenger approached him beseechingly, stating that the pasha would give a hundred pounds if he was landed that night.

"I would not attempt such a thing for twenty hundred," said the captain.

"Will nothing tempt you, then, to run a risk?" asked the interpreter.

"Nothing but the clearing away of the fog," replied the commander.

He then commenced to walk the bridge, and pondered over the experience he was having, wrestling with himself as to the amount of risk he should run. He called the second officer to him, and gave him orders to go aloft to the foretopgallant mast-head and see if he could make anything out. The officer was in the act of jumping into the rigging when a Turkish schooner sailed close alongside and was soon out of sight. The captain knew then that he was in the vicinity of the entrance, and set the engines easy ahead. The second mate, after being at the mast-head about ten minutes, shouted —

"I see over the top of the fog a lighthouse or tower on the port bow. I can see no land."

When he was asked if he could see anything on the starboard bow, his answer came in the negative. The captain, fearing lest he might be steering into the false Bosphorus, which is a treacherous deep bight that has been the death-trap of many a ship's crew, gave orders to stop her while he ran aloft to verify the officer's report and scan over the mist for some landmark to guide him in navigating in the right direction. He had only been a few minutes at the mast-head when he discerned the white lighthouse on the starboard bow. There was no doubt now that these were the Bosphorus lighthouses, and the vessel was heading right for the centre. The captain asked if they could see anything from the deck. The chief mate replied that he could scarcely see the forecastle head, so dense was the fog. The master shouted that he would navigate the steamer from the topgallant-yard, and gave instructions to go slow ahead, and to keep a vigilant look-out for passing vessels. Half an hour's steaming brought them abreast of the lighthouses, when suddenly they glided into beautiful, clear weather. The scene was phenomenal. Not a speck of fog was to be seen ahead of the vessel, while astern there stood a great black pall, as though one had drawn a curtain across the harbour entrance.

After the papers had been landed at Kavak, the pasha and interpreter came to the bridge and asked for a few minutes' talk with the captain, who was in excellent temper at having cut through the fog and saved daylight through the narrow waters. The pasha was dressed gorgeously, and many decorations adorned his uniform. He shook the proud commander warmly by the hand, and through his interpreter gratefully thanked him for carrying himself and his suite safely to their destination. He did not undervalue the great danger of having them aboard in the event of being chased and captured, nor did he under-estimate the risk that had been run in steaming into dangerous waters during a dense fog; and in order that the captain might be assured of his grateful appreciation, he begged to hand him two hundred Turkish pounds for himself. After suitably offering his thanks for so generous a gift, the captain again asked the interpreter the name of the distinguished general he had had the honour of carrying as a passenger, and was again told that such questions could not be answered.

Before the sun had sunk beneath the horizon, they had reached Scutari; and in order that the passengers might be disembarked comfortably, the anchor was dropped. Caiques came alongside for them and for their baggage. The captain went to the gangway to see the pasha safely into the boat, and to say his *adieux* to him. After he had got safely seated in the caique, and the interpreter was about to follow, the commander held out his hand to him and said—

"Before bidding good-bye, may I again venture to ask if I have had the honour of conveying Osman Pasha to Constantinople, or whom I have conveyed?"

The interpreter, with an air of injured pride, drew himself up to his full height, and said—

"Captain, I have told you not to ask such things. Good-day."

But that was how one of the heroes of Plevna made his first English ally by sea.

A Russian Port in the 'Sixties

My first visit to Russia was at the age of thirteen. I was serving aboard a smart brig that had just come from the Guano Islands in the Indian Ocean. The captain and officers belonged to the "swell" type of seaman of that period. The former has just passed away at the age of eighty-four. He was in his younger days a terror to those who served under him, and a despot who knew no pity. In an ordinary way he was most careful not to lower the dignity of his chief officer in the eyes of the crew, but wherever his self-interest was concerned he did not stick at trivialities. I have a vivid recollection of a very picturesque passage of words being exchanged between him and his first mate. The officer had been commanded to go ashore in the longboat at 5 a.m. on the morning after arrival for the labourers who were required to assist the sailors to discharge the cargo. The infuriated mate asked his commander if he took him for a "procurator" of Russian serfs, and reminded him that his certificate of competency was a qualification for certain duties which he was willing to perform; but as this did not come within the scope of them, he would see him to blazes before he would stoop to the level of becoming the engager of a drove of Russian convicts.

"What is it coming to," said he, "that a chief mate should be requested to take charge of a boat-load of fellows who wouldn't be fit to live in our country? The boatswain is the proper man to do this kind of work, and if you cannot trust him to select the lousie rascals, then go yourself!"

These harsh words affected the captain so much that he became inarticulate with passion; but when he had somewhat recovered, the splendour of his jerky vocabulary could be heard far beyond the precincts of the cabin. He declared that his authority had never been outraged in such a fashion before, and with the air of an autocrat ordered the mate to his berth until the morrow, when he would have to appear before the British Consul.

The officer's pride was injured, his temper was up, and he began to suitably libel everybody. Her Majesty's representative was the object of much vituperation, and a rather brilliant harangue was brought to a close by the officer stating that he would go and see the blooming Consul, and say some straight things to him. With a final flourish he called out at the top of his voice, disdainfully—

"Who the h— — is he?"

The next morning at ten o'clock the captain gave orders to row him ashore. The mate wore a humbler appearance than on the previous day: meditation had mellowed him. He stepped into the boat beside his commander, but was told with icy dignity that the boy would take him ashore in the cook's lurky. No greater insult could have been offered to an officer. The Consul at that time was Walter Maynard, a charming man whom I knew well years afterwards. Although I only heard odds and ends of what transpired, I feel sure the advice given was in the mate's interests, and made him see his objection from another point of view. He did not take kindly to bringing the labourers off, but he sullenly commenced from that day to do it.

Coal cargoes were at that time jumped out of the hold with four ropes bent on to one called a runner, which was rove through a coal gin fastened on to the end of a derrick composed of two studdingsail booms lashed together, and steps were rigged with studdingsail yards and oars. The arrangement had the appearance of a gate, and was fixed at an angle. Four men gave one sharp pull with the whip ropes, and then jumped from the step on to the deck. The men in the hold changed places with the whips every two hours. It was really an exciting thing to witness the whipping out of coal cargoes. It may be seen even now in some ports of the United Kingdom, but the winch has largely taken the place of this athletic process. Most captains supplied rum or vodka liberally, with a view to expediting dispatch, and did not scruple to log and fine those seamen who acquired a craving for alcohol, and misconducted themselves in consequence when they got liberty to go ashore. Nobody was more severe on the men who committed a breach of discipline than those who, for their own profit, had taught them to drink.

The poor, wretched Russians who were employed aboard English and other vessels were treated with a cruelty that was hideous. Before the emancipation of the serfs by the Emperor Alexander II. in 1861, it was not an uncommon occurrence for captains and officers and seamen to maltreat them, knock them on the head, and then pass their bodies over the side of the vessel into the Mole. One of the first things I remember hearing in a Russian port was a savage mate swearing at some labourers and threatening to throw them overboard. It is no exaggeration to say that almost every day dead bodies came to the surface and were taken to the "Bran" Wharf or to the mortuary, with never a word of inquiry as to how they came by their end, though it was well known that there had been foul play. It is true they were awful thieves, very dirty, very lazy, and very provoking, and it was because the officers were unable to get redress that they took the law into their own hands. It is incredible that such a condition of things was allowed to exist.

A stock phrase even to this day of predatory Russians is, "Knet crawlim, tackem"—*i.e.*, "I have not stolen, I have only taken." They have a pronounced conviction that there is a difference between stealing and taking. Tradition has it that a humorous seaman ages ago conveyed this form of distinction to them, and it has stuck to them ever since. Another peculiarity of the race is that they wear the same large grey coat in the summer as they do in the winter; they are taught to believe that what keeps out cold keeps out heat. When they take drink they never stop until they are dead drunk, then they lie anywhere about the streets and quays. The police, who are not much better, use them very cruelly. During the Russo-Turkish war hundreds of the common soldiers, who are similar to the common labourer, were found lying on the battle-field, presumably dead, when it was found they were only dead drunk. I was told by a doctor, who went right through the campaign, that it was customary to fill the "soldads," as they are called, previous to a battle, with vodka. The lower order of Russians must be hardy, or they could never stand the extremes of cold and heat, and the terrible food they have to eat. They are not long-lived. I cannot recall ever having seen a very old Russian labourer.

The emancipation of the serfs was a great grievance to the old seamen, who looked back to the days when they could with impunity chastise or finish a serf without a feeling of reproach. After the emancipation it became a terror to have them aboard ship. Many a mate has been heavily fined and locked up in a pestilential cell for merely shoving a fellow who was caught in the act of stealing, or found skulking, or deliberately refusing to work properly. Labourers, in fact, became a herd of blackmailers, and were encouraged in it by some agency or other, who shared the plunder. One old captain, with an expression of sadness on his face, told me, on my first visit to Cronstadt since I was a boy, that everything had changed for the worse.

"At one time," said he, "you never got up of a morning without seeing a few dead Russians floating about. You could chuck them overboard if you liked, and nobody interfered. Many a time I've put one over the side. But now you dare not whisper, much less touch them."

The general opinion amongst English seamen, from the master downwards, was that a great injustice had been done to us by the Decree of Liberation.

On one occasion I lay alongside a Yankee ship which was loading flax. Work had ceased for breakfast. I saw the chief officer on the poop, said "Good morning" to him, and asked him how the loading was going on.

"Well," said he, "it goes not so bad, but we've had an accident this morning which stopped us for nearly an hour. There were three or four bales of flax slung in the hatchway; the slings slipped, and the bales fell right on a dozen Russians."

"That is very serious," I said. "Did it kill them?"

"No," drawled he, with a slow smile; "it didn't exactly kill them, but I guess it has flattened them out some."

The "Bran" Wharf was then a large pontoon, with dwelling accommodation for Custom-house officers and harbour officials. It was moored just at the entrance to the dock or mole, and was in charge of an official who regulated the berthing of vessels. This man was originally a boatswain aboard a Russian warship. He was illiterate, but very clever, so much so that great power was put into his hands; indeed, he became quite as powerful in his way as his Imperial Majesty himself. Every conceivable complaint and petty dispute was taken to him, and it was soon found that it could be settled in a way that did not involve a fine or imprisonment. In fact, there were occasions when a favourite English captain or mate asked this official's aid in getting the Russians to work properly. He would, if agreeably disposed, come aboard, spit, stamp, and swear at the men in a most picturesque way, and if he had had a glass or two of grog, or wanted one, and the captain or mate made a very bad report, he would lash the skulkers with a piece of rope. When he was finished there was no more need for complaint. This notorious person was called Tom the Boatswain. He drew very fine distinctions as to whom he favoured with his countenance and his chastening rod. For obvious reasons, he loathed a Swede and a Norwegian. In truth, he told me himself that Englishmen were "dobra" (good), and that Norwegians and Swedes were "knet dobra." He spoke a peculiar kind of English, with a fascinating accent, and when he went his rounds in the early morning, rowed by two uniformed sailors, studied respect was paid to him. His invitations to breakfast, or to have a glass of brandy (which he preferred to whisky), indicated the esteem, fear, or amount of favours inspired by him. He in turn endeavoured to pay a hurried visit to each of his guests, ostensibly to see that their vessels were properly berthed, and the men working properly, but really to test the generosity of the captains, who seldom let him go without a "douceur," which was sometimes satisfactory. He was accustomed, when asked to have refreshment, to request that his two men should have a nip also. One morning he visited a favourite captain who had arranged with his mate to act liberally towards the men. His stay in the cabin was prolonged, and when he came on deck and called for the boat, his devoted henchmen did not come forth. He looked over the quarter-deck, and was thrown into frenzy by seeing them both lying speechless, their bodies in the bottom, and their legs sticking up on the seats of the boat. He got into her, kicked the two occupants freely without producing from them any appreciable symptoms of life, and then finally rowed himself back to the "Bran" Wharf. The two culprits were compulsory teetotalers after that.

Their master went on accumulating roubles, which, under Russian law, Tom could not invest in his own name, and perhaps he had personal reasons for secrecy. He did not allow the amount of his wealth to be known to gentlemen who might have relieved him of the anxiety of watching over it. But, alas! there came a period of great trial to Tom. That portion of the "Bran" Wharf where the roubles were concealed took fire. The occupants had to fly for their lives, and soon the whole fabric was burnt to the water's edge. Another pontoon was erected in its place, and Tom put in command; but before he had time to replace the fortune he had lost, he was superseded by a naval officer, and his roubles were taken from him. I believe his dismissal was brought about by one of the countrymen to whom he had such a strong aversion making a complaint to the Governor about his partiality to Englishmen. Great sympathy was secretly extended to poor Tom by his English friends, but the loss of his position and his wealth broke his heart, and he only survived the blow for a few weeks.

In addition to controlling the berthing of vessels, and keeping the harbour free from confusion, it was Tom's duty to see that no fires or lights were allowed either by day or night, and, as these rigid rules were frequently broken, his "hush money" very largely contributed to his already affluent income. Nor did his removal affect the acquisitiveness of his successor, who loyally followed in his footsteps. As soon as a sailing-vessel arrived in the Roads, the galley fire had to be put out before she was allowed to come into the Mole. All cooking was done ashore at a cookhouse that was loathsomely dirty. A heavy charge was made for the use of the place, and also for the hire of the cook's lurky, a flat-bottomed kind of boat constructed of rough planks. These boats were invariably so leaky that on the passage to and from the shore they became half-foil of water, and the food was frequently spoiled in consequence. But, even if all went right, the crews often had to partake of badly cooked, cold rations. Many a meal was lost altogether, and once or twice a poor cook who could not swim was drowned by the boat filling and capsizing. The frail craft of this kind were of curious shape, and only a person who had the knack could row them. No more comical sport could be witnessed than the lurky race which was held every season. Many of the cooks never acquired the art of rowing straight, and whenever they put a spurt on the lurky would run amuck in consequence of being flat-bottomed and having no keel. Then the carnival of collisions, capsizing of boats, and rescuing of their occupants began. Some disdained assistance, and heroically tried to right their erratic "dug-outs." It would be impossible to draw a true picture of these screamingly funny incidents, but be it remembered they were all sailor-cooks who took part in the sport, and the riotous joy they derived therefrom was always a pleasant memory, and kept them for days in good temper for carrying out the pilgrimage to and from the cookhouse.

The popular English idea is that there are only two classes in Russia — viz., the upper and lower; but this is quite a mistake. There has always been a thrifty shopkeeping and artisan class, which may be called their middle lower class. Then there is a class that comes between them and the common labourer. Nearly all the shopkeepers that carry on business at Cronstadt, Riga, and other Northern Russian ports during the summer have their real homes in Moscow, and mostly all speak a little English. There are also the boatmen, who are a well-behaved, well-dressed lot of men, whose homes are in Archangel. They, as well as the tradesmen, come every spring, and leave when the port closes in the autumn. In the sailing-ship days each of the greengrocers — as they were called, though they sold all kinds of stores besides — had their connection. Every afternoon, between four and six, batches of captains were to be found seated in a greengrocer's shop having a glass of tea with a piece of lemon in it. It was then they spun their yarns in detail about their passages, their owners, their mates, their crews, and their loading and discharging. If their vessels were unchartered they discussed that too, but whenever they got authority from their owners to charter on the best possible terms they became reticent and sly with each other. To exchange views as to the rate that should be accepted would have been regarded as a decided token of business incapacity. Supposing two captains had their vessels unchartered, each would give instructions to be called early in the morning, that they might go in the first boat to St. Petersburg, and neither would know what the other intended. When they met aboard the passenger boat they would lie to each other grotesquely about what was taking them to town. If they were unsuccessful in fixing, they rarely disclosed what had been offered; and this would go on for days, until they had to fix; then they would draw closer to each other, and relate in the most minute fashion the history of all the negotiations, and how cleverly they had gained this or that advantage over the charterers; whereas, in truth, their agents or brokers had great trouble in getting some of them to understand the precise nature of the business that was being negotiated. The following is an instance.

Mr. James Young, of South Shields, whose many vessels were distinguished by having a frying-pan at the foretopgallant or royal masthead, had a brig at Cronstadt which had been waiting unloaded for some days. Her master was one of the old illiterate class. His peace of mind was much disturbed at Mr. Young's indifference. At last he got a telegram asking him to wire the best freights offering. He proceeded to St. Petersburg, bounced into Mr. Charles Maynard's office, and introduced himself as Mark Gaze, one of Jimmy Young's skippers.

"Well," said Mr. Maynard, in his polite way, "and what can I do for you, Captain Gaze?"

"Dee for me, sorr? Wire the aad villain that she's been lyin' a week discharged."

"Yes," said the broker, writing down something very different. "And what else?"

"Tell him," said Mark, "te fetch the aad keel back te the Gut, and let hor lie and rot wheor he can see hor!"

"Very good," said Maynard, still waiting; "and what else?"

"Whaat else? Oh, tell him to gan to h— —, and say Mark Gaze says see. Ask him whaat the blazes he means be runnin' the risk of gettin' hor frozzen in. Say aa'll seun be at Shields owerland, if he dizzen't mind whaat he's aboot."

"Well, now," said the agent, "I think we have got to the bottom of things. We'll send this telegram off; but before it goes, would you like me to read it to you?"

"For God's sake send the d— — thing away!" said Mark. "And tell him te come and tyek the aad beast hyem hissel; or, if he likes, aa'll run hor on te Hogland for him."

"Well, you do seem to understand your owner and speak plainly to him. I should think he knows he has got an excellent master who looks after his interest."

"Interest! What diz he knaa aboot interest? He knaas mair aboot the West Docks. Understand him, d'ye say? If aa divvent, thor's neebody in his employ diz. Aa've been forty-five years wiv him and his fethor tegithor. Aa sarved me time wiv him. He dorsent say a word, or aa'd tell him to take his ship to h— — wiv him."

"That is really capital," said the much amused agent. "Now, what do you say, captain, if we have some light refreshment and a cigar?"

"Ay, that's what aa caal business. But aa nivvor tyek leet refreshment. Ma drink is brandy or whisky neat," said Captain Gaze, his face beaming with good-nature.

They proceeded to a restaurant, and when they got nicely settled down with their drinks and smokes, the skipper remarked—

"Aa wonder what Jimmie waad say if he could see Mark Gaze sittin' in a hotel hevvin' his whisky and smokin' a cigar?"

"I should think," said Mr. Maynard, "he would raise your wages, or give you command of a larger ship." And then there was hearty laughter.

Captain Gaze had a profound dislike to Russians, and more than once narrowly escaped severe punishment for showing it. I have often heard him swearing frightfully at the men passing deals from the lighters into the bow ports of his vessel, and declaring that God Almighty must have had little on hand when he put them on earth. Certainly he would have considered it an act of gross injustice if, having killed or drowned any of them, he had been punished for it.

Mark did not know anything about history that was written in books. He only knew that which had occurred in his own time, and the crude bits he had heard talked of amongst his own class. He, and those who were his shipmates and contemporaries during the Russian War, believed that a great act of cowardice and bad treatment had been committed in not allowing Charlie Napier to blow the forts down and take possession of Cronstadt. [2] They knew nothing of the circumstances that led to the withdrawal of the fleet, but their inherent belief was that a dirty trick had been served on Charlie, and Russians, irrespective of class, were told whenever an opportunity occurred, that they should never neglect to thank Heaven that the British Government was so generous as to refrain from blowing them into space.

At Cronstadt, after the introduction of steam, it became a custom for stevedores' runners, and representatives and vendors of other commodities, to have their boats outside the Mole at three and four o'clock in the morning during the summer. The captain of each vessel, as soon as she was slowed down or anchored, was canvassed vigorously by each of the competitors. One morning, the representative of Deal Yard No. 6, who was an ex-English captain, came into sharp conflict with a Russian competitor. The latter rudely interrupted the ex-captain while he was complimenting a friend who had just arrived on having made a smart passage. All captains like to be told they have made a smart passage, but the ardent advocate of Deal Yard No. 6 kept welcoming his friend at great length, obviously to prevent the other runners from getting a word at the new arrival. There arose a revolt against him, headed by a person who was always supposed to be a Russian, but who spoke English more correctly than his English competitor. The ex-captain was somewhat corpulent. He was short, and had a plump, good-natured face which suggested that he was not a bigoted teetotaler; he had a suit of clothes on that did not convey the idea of a West-end tailor; his dialect was broad Yorkshire, and his conversational capacity interminable. The representative of No. 10 Deal Yard undertook to stop his flow of rhetoric by calling out, "Stop it, old baggy breeches! Give other people a chance!" But he paid no heed, and did not even break the thread of his talk until the captain of the steamer began to walk towards the companion-way, when he stopped short and said, "Well, I suppose I'm to book you for No. 6?" and then there was a clamour. The whole of the runners wished to get their word in before the captain definitely promised, but they were too late. No. 6 had got it; but instead of accepting his success modestly, he was so elated at having taken away an order from another yard, that he stood up in his boat and congratulated himself on being an Englishman.

"No use you fellows coming off here when I'm awake; and, you bet, I'm always awake when there's any Muscovite backstairs gentlemen about."

As the boats were being rowed into the Mole again, some one asked who had got the ship. The Russian competitor, who was angry at the work being taken from his master, called out, "Bags has got her, the drunken old sneak!"

Bags lost no time in letting fly an oar at him, the yoke and rudder quickly following. His vengeance was let loose, and he poured forth a stream of quarter-deck language at the top of his voice. His phrases were dazzling in ingenuity, and amid much laughter and applause he urged his hearers to keep at a distance from the fellow who had dared to insult an English shipmaster.

"Or you will get some passengers that will keep you busy. They—*he*— calls them *peoches*, but we English call them *lice!*"

This sally caused immense amusement, not so much for what was said as for his dramatic style of saying it. His antagonist retorted that he had been turned out of England for bad language and bad behaviour, and he would have him turned out of Russia also. This nearly choked the old mariner with rage. He roared out—

"Did I, an English shipmaster, ever think that I would come to this, to be insulted by a Russian serf? I will let the Government know that an

Englishman has been insulted. I will lay the iniquities of this Russian system of rascality before Benjamin Disraeli. I knows him; and if he is the man I takes him for, he won't stand any nonsense when it comes to insulting English subjects. He has brought the Indian troops from India for that purpose, and when the honour of England is at stake he will send the fleet into the Baltic, and neither your ships nor your forts will prevent his orders to blow Cronstadt down about your blooming ears being carried out. I know where your torpedoes and mines are, and Disraeli has confidence in me showing them the road to victory. The British Lion never draws back!"

The Russian deal-yard man, to whom this harangue was particularly directed, went to the Governor on landing, and stated what the rough, weather-beaten old sailor had been saying. The Governor communicated with the authorities at St. Petersburg, and an order came to have the old Englishman banished from Cronstadt and Russia for ever within twenty-four hours. The poor creature had made a home for himself in Cronstadt, his wife and four children being with him. The blow was so sharp and unexpected, it stupefied him. His first thought was his family, but there was little or no time for thought or preparation. He had either to be got away or concealed. A liberal distribution of roubles at the instigation of many sympathizers made it possible for him to be put aboard an English steamer, and a week after his banishment was supposed to have taken effect he sailed from Cronstadt, a ruined and broken-hearted man. The old sailor's grief for the harm his wayward conduct had done to his wife and family was quite pathetic, and so far as kindness could appease the mental anguish he was having to endure it was ungrudgingly extended to him, and when he left Cronstadt he left behind him a host of sympathizers who regarded the punishment as odious.

The fact of any public official listening to a miscreant who told the story of a stevedores' row, to which he himself had been a party, and seriously believing that the threats, however extravagant and bellicose, of a verbose old sailor could be a national danger, is, on the face of it, so ludicrous that the English reader may easily doubt the accuracy of such an incident; and yet it is true.

In other days I used occasionally to meet members of the Russian revolutionary party at my brother's home in London. They were all men and women of education and refinement. The first time I met them the late Robert Louis Stevenson (who generally used the window as a means of exit instead of the door), William Henley, George Collins (editor of the *Schoolmaster*), and, I think, Mr. Wright (author of *the Journeyman Engineer*) were there. The talk was very brilliant. My brother, who was a charming conversationalist, kept his visitors fascinated with anecdotes about Carlyle and John Ruskin, whom he knew well. They spoke, too, about the unsigned articles which they were each contributing to a paper called the *London*, and their criticism of each other's work was very lively. But to me the most touching incident of the afternoon was the story told by one of the revolutionary party about Sophie Peroffsky, who mounted the scaffold with four of her friends, kissed and encouraged them with cheering words until the time came that they should be executed. He related also a touching and detailed story of little Marie Soubitine, who refused to purchase her own safety by uttering a word to betray her friends, and was kept lingering in an underground dungeon for three years, at the end of which she was sent off to Siberia, and died on the road. No amount of torture could make her betray her friends. They spoke of Antonoff, who was subjected to the thumbscrew, had red-hot wires thrust under his nails, and when his torturers gave him a little respite he would scratch on his plate cipher signals to his comrades.

The account of the cause and origin of the revolutionary movement and its subsequent history, which sparkled with heroic deeds, was told in a quiet, unostentatious manner. I had just come from Russia. I had been much in that country, and thought I knew a great deal about it and the sinister system of government that breeds revolutionaries; but the tales of cruel, senseless despotism told by these people made me shudder with horror. I had been accustomed to abhor and look upon Nihilists as a scoundrelly gang of lawless butchers, but I found them the most cultured of patriots, loving their country, though detesting the barbarous system of government which had driven them and thousands of their compatriots from the land and friends they loved, and from the estates they owned, into resigned and determined agitation for popular government and the amelioration of their people. The upholders of this despotic system of government are now engaged in a life-and-death struggle, and all civilized nations are looking forward to the time when, for the first time in its history, Right and not Might shall prevail in Russia. It has been said, "Happy is the nation that has no history." Russia knows this to her cost, for her history is being made every day, with all the horrible accompaniments of massacres, injustice, and tyranny. Only it should be remembered that the fight must be between tyranny and liberty, and that the Russian peasant must work out his own salvation. This may be—nay, must be—the work of years, but England's sympathy will be with the workers for freedom. English feeling on the matter was well expressed by the statesman who had the courage to say publicly, "Long live the Duma!" and every Englishman will in his heart of hearts applaud any efforts made to secure constitutional government.

FOOTNOTES

[2] Napier was a great favourite with his sailors, notwithstanding his apparent harshness to them at times. Whenever he wanted a dash made on a strong position, he inspired them with a fury of enthusiasm by giving the word of command incisively, and then adding as an addendum, "Now, off you go, you damned rascals, and exterminate them." This was a form of endearment, and they knew it.

"Dutchy" and his Chief

A handsome barque lay at the quay of a South Wales port, ready to sail, and waiting only for the flood tide. Her name was the *Pacific*, and she was commanded by a person of laborious dignity. His officers were selected to meet the tastes and ambitions of their captain, whose name was John Kickem. I have said before it was customary in those days for crowds of people to congregate on the quays or dock sides to watch the departure of vessels. Some came out of curiosity, but many were the relatives and friends of different members of the crew who wished to say their *adieux*, and to listen to the sombre singing of the chanties as the men mastheaded the topsail yards, or catted and fished the anchors. These vessels were known as copper-ore-men. They were usually manned with picked able seamen and three apprentices. In this instance they were all fine specimens of English manhood. It was no ordinary sight to witness the display of bunting as it stretched from royal truck to rail, and the grotesque love-making of the seafarers as they hugged and kissed their wives and sweethearts over and over again with amazing rapidity. One of the favourite songs which they delighted to sing on such auspicious occasions was rendered with touching pathos—

> "Sing good-bye to Sal, and good-bye to Sue;
> Away Rio!
> And you that are list'ning, good-bye to you;
> For we're bound to Rio Grande!
> And away Rio, aye Rio!
> Sing fare ye well, my bonny young girl,
> We're bound to Rio Grande."

It didn't matter, of course, where they were bound to, this ditty was the farewell song; and it always had the desired effect of melting the bystanders, especially the females, though Jack himself showed no really soft emotion. Not that they were not sentimental, but theirs seemed always to be a frolicsome sentimentality.

The eldest apprentice of the *Pacific* was in his eighteenth year. He was a fine, broad-shouldered, fair-haired, medium-sized youth. He had been dividing his attentions amongst a number of girl admirers, and was told to come aboard to unmoor and give the tug the tow-rope. While these orders were being carried out the lad caught sight of a young girl who had just arrived in a great state of excitement. She was dressed in dazzling finery, and carrying something in a basket. The boy sprang on to the dock wall, and created much merriment with his elephantine caresses. They shouted to him from the vessel to jump aboard or he would lose his passage. He made a running spring for the main rigging as she was being towed from her berth. A wild cheer went up from the crowd when they saw the smart thing that had been done, and that he was safe. The devoted female who had caused him to dare so much, in the luxuriance of grief, shouted to him —

"Good-bye, Jim! You've always been a rare good pal to a girl. Take care of yourself; and mind, no sweethearts at every port!" The latter communication was made almost inarticulate with sobbing. Her last words were, "Don't forget, Jim!" To which he replied, "You bet, I won't!"

Soon the attractive craft, and her equally attractive crew were lost sight of amidst the haze of the gathering night. A quiet, easterly air wa fitfully blowing in the Channel, and when full sail was set, the pilot ar tug left. All night she trailed sinuously over the peaceful sea, and as the cold dawn was breaking she slid past the south end of Lundy Island with a freshening breeze at her stern. In a few days the north-east trade winds which blow gently over the bosom of the ocean were reached, and every stitch of canvas was hung up. The sailors had got over their monotony, and began to entertain themselves during the dog-watches from six to eight. The imperious commander was never happy himself, and was angry at the sight of mirth in anybody. He forthwith commenced a system that was well calculated to breed revolt, and which did ultimately do so. Orders were given that there were to be no afternoon watches below, and all hands were to be kept at work until 6 p.m. In addition to this petty tyranny, the crew were put on their bare whack of everything, including water; and so the dreary days and nights passed on until Cape Horn was reached. They had long realized that the burden of their song should be "Good-day, bad day, God send Sunday." The weather was stormy off the Horn, and nearly a month was spent in fruitless attempts to get round. The spirit had been knocked out of the officers and crew by senseless bullying and wicked persecution. They had no heart left to put into their work, otherwise the vessel would have got past this boisterous region in half the time. At last she arrived at Iquique, and, like all ill-conditioned creatures who have been born wrong and have polecat natures, the captain blamed the hapless officers and crew for the long passage, and in order to punish the poor innocent fellows, he refused to them both money and liberty to go ashore. Treatment of such a character could only have one ending — and that was mutiny, if not murder;

and yet this senseless fellow, in defiance of all human law, kept on goading them to it. He was warned by a catspaw (whom even despised bullies can have in their pay) that the forecastle was a hotbed of murderous intent, and that for his own safety he should give the men liberty to go ashore, and advance them what money they required.

"Let them revolt!" said he. "I will soon have them where they deserve to be, the rascals. Let them, if they dare, disturb me in my cabin, and I'll riddle them with lead. If they want to go ashore, let them go without liberty; but if they do, their wages will be forfeited, and I will have them put in prison."

A policy of this kind was the more remarkable, as even if the men were driven to desertion it was impossible to fill their places at anything like the same wages, or with the same material. The available hands were either not sailors at all, or if they were, they belonged to the criminal class that feared neither God nor man, and knew no law or pity except that which was unto themselves. On the other hand, this vessel was manned with the cream of British seamen, who would have dared anything for their captain and owners had they been treated as was their right. He had run the length of human forbearance. The crew struck. They demanded to see the British Consul, and submit their grievances to him. Sometimes this authority is but a poor tribunal to appeal to when real discrimination is to be determined. On this occasion the seamen were fortunate in getting a sympathetic verdict, and the captain got what he deserved—a good trouncing for his treatment of them. They were willing to sign off the articles, and he was plainly told that they must either be paid their wages in full, or he undertake to carry out the conditions of engagement in a proper manner. "And I must warn you," said the irate official of the British Government, "if you drive these men out of your ship, you may expect no assistance from me in collecting another crew. The men are right, and you are wrong."

The captain was in a state of sullen passion at the turn things had taken against him. He said that he would decide the following day whether the proper course for him to take, now that his authority had been broken, was to pay the men off or not. On the morrow he intimated his decision to pay them off. Poor creature, it would have been well for him and all connected with this doomed vessel had he swallowed his pride and resolved to behave in a rational way to his crew. The places of respectable men were filled with human reptiles of various nationalities—criminals, every one of them. He must have persuaded himself that his despotism would have fuller play with these foreigners, whose savage vengeance was destined to shock the whole civilized world with their awful butchery. The apprentices and officers did not take kindly to the changed condition of things. They instinctively felt that they were to become associated with a gang of -, and hoped that something would transpire to prevent this happening. An opportunity was given the oldest apprentice in an unexpected way. The captain had ordered his gig to be ashore to take him aboard at a certain time at night. The boat was there before the captain, and as he was so long in coming the boat's crew went for a walk ashore. The great man came down and had to wait a few minutes for his men. This caused him to become abusive, which the oldest apprentice, James Leigh, resented by using some longshore adjectives. The master seized the foothold of the stroke oar and threw it at the lad, and when they got aboard the captain again attempted to strike him, but the lad let fly, and did considerable damage in a rough and tumble way to the bully, who was now like a wild beast. James was ultimately overpowered and got a bad beating. He thereupon determined to run away, and he laid his plans accordingly. In a few days he was far away from the sea in a safe, hospitable hiding-place, with some friends who knew his family at home, and the *Pacific* had sailed long before he reached the coast again.

After a few months' travelling about, picking up jobs here and there, he was brought in contact with a rich old Spaniard who owned a leaky old barque which was employed in the coasting trade. The captain of her was a Dutchman who spoke English very imperfectly, and what he did know was spoken with a nasal Yankee twang. It was a habit, as well as being thought an accomplishment in those days, as it is in these, to affect American dialect and adopt their slang and mannerisms in order to convey an impression of importance. Even a brief visit to the country, or a single passage in a Yankee ship was sufficient to turn a hitherto humble fellow into an insufferable imitator. It was obvious the skipper had been a good deal on the Spanish Main, as he spoke their language with a fluency that left no doubt as to what he had been doing for many years. He was discovered at a time when the owner was in much need of some one to take charge of his vessel, as she did not attract the highest order of captain. The Dutchman had no Board of Trade master or mate certificate; he was merely a sailor. James Leigh was discovered in pretty much the same way as the captain, and the owner took a strong liking to him at the outset. He was good to look at, and gifted with a bright intelligence which made him attractive, besides having the advantage of knowing something about navigation. The chief mate's berth was offered to him and accepted. Furthermore, it was suggested that he should visit and stay at the owner's house, whenever the vessel was in port and his services were not required aboard, and seeing that he was not yet eighteen, he felt flattered at the distinction that had been thrust upon him. Perhaps he accepted the invitation all the more readily as he was informed by his employer that he had two daughters that would like to make his acquaintance.

The first voyage was to Coronel and back with coal to Iquique. Mr. Leigh, as he was now addressed by everybody, on the ship or ashore, had intimated to his commander that he liked his berth for the prospects that might open up to him, but he didn't relish the thought of having to pump so continuously; whereupon Captain Vandertallen winked hard at him, and strongly urged that it should be put up with, and to keep his eye on the girls who were to inherit their father's fortune.

"I tink," said he, "I vill marry de one and you vill have de other."

"I don't know about that," retorted James Leigh. "You see I've a girl at home, and somehow I thinks a lot about her. But a bit of money makes a difference; I must think it over."

Quarterdeck etiquette was not observed between the two men. The captain addressed his first officer as Jim, and Jim addressed his captain as "Dutchy." This familiarity was arrived at soon after they came together, owing to a strong difference of opinion on some point of seamanship which had to do with the way a topgallant sail ought to be taken in without running any risk of splitting it. The quarrel was furious. Jim had called his commander "a blithering, fat-headed Dutchman, not fit to have charge of a dung barge, much less a square-rigged ship. Captain Kickem of the *Pacific* would not have carried you as ballast."

Vandertallen was almost inarticulate. He frothed out—

"Yes, an' you he vould not carry at all; you too much chick. Remember I the captain, and I vill discharge you at first port."

"Oh, you go to h——!"

"No, I vill not go to h——. I'll just stay here, and you can go to ----. You jist a boy."

"All right, Dutchy," replied the refractory mate; "you'll want me before I want you."

And this was a correct prediction, as, a few days later, Dutchy lost himself, and was obliged to come to his mate and ask the true position of the vessel.

"I am not captain," said he. "Do it yourself; you are a very clever fellow."

"No, no," said Vandertallen; "you know better dan me. Let us be friends, Jim. I call you Jim; you call me Dutchy, or vat you like."

"All right, then," said James Leigh. "If that is to be the way, I'll tell you where you are, and if you had run in the same direction other four hours you would have been ashore on the Island of Mocha."

"Vair is dat?" said Vandertallen, nervously.

"For Heaven's sake don't ask such silly questions," said the mate. "You are miles out of your reckoning."

"Vell, I'm d——!" said the amazed skipper. "Den you must do de reckonin' now, Jim."

"That's all very well, Dutchy, but if I have to do the navigation I am entitled to share the pay."

"Vary vell," replied his captain, "dat agree."

So henceforth they were co-partners in everything—wages, perquisites, and position; and they never again got out of their reckoning. It was obvious James was first favourite with the crew, and after the first voyage the veteran owner showed his marked approval. Jim was allowed to do just as he pleased. The daughters were charmed with him, and frequently visited the vessel with their father when the officers could not get conveniently to their home. A strong and growing attachment was quite apparent so far as the girls were concerned. There seemed to be a preference with both of them for the first mate, who, in turn, fixed his affections on the youngest. His comrade was not quite satisfied with being so frequently ignored, so remonstrated with Jim to stick to one, and he would stick to the other; but the ladies having to be taken into account, it did not work at all smoothly, as each desired to have Mr. Leigh, and before it was settled the sisters had a violent tiff, which brought about the climax and made it possible for negotiations to be carried on in favour of a settlement. The father selected the elder girl for Vandertallen, and the younger was fixed on Leigh, who threw himself into the vortex of flirtation with youthful ardour. He thought at one time of marrying and settling down in Chili, and undoubtedly the owner and daughter gave encouragement to this idea.

But letters began to arrive from home, which had an unsettling effect on him. He was afraid to give his confidence to the captain lest he might break faith with him, but in truth his mind and heart were centred on a picturesque spot on the side of a Welsh hill, and in that little home there was one who longed to have him back. Indeed, she had written to say that if he did not come soon to her she would come to him. These communications revived all the old feelings of affection in his breast, and he resolved to tear himself away from the environment which had gripped him like a vice. The old Spaniard kept hinting marriage to him each time he paid a visit to the superb villa, but he refused to be drawn into anything definite. As he said—

"The place is getting too hot for me. I must face it sooner or later if I am not to permanently settle in Chili. Once married it is all over with me.

I will have loads of money, but am I sure it will bring happiness? I think I must say that I lean towards a daughter of my native land, who may not have wealth, but who has all the attributes that appeal to me. In a few days I must decide."

These were some of the thoughts occupying Jim's mind as the leaky old ark lounged her way along the coast. The captain, on the other hand, talked freely to his mate as to his own thoughts, prompted no doubt by close companionship and the idea of becoming brothers-in-law. He told Leigh that both of them would be very wealthy some day, but Jim kept his counsel. He had resolved that if the subject was mentioned by the Spaniard again he would make himself scarce.

On their arrival at Iquique, Leigh received more letters from home. He went to the owner's house, and in the course of the evening the old gentleman asked him right out to marry his daughter. Mr. Leigh was confused, and said he would like to save a little more money.

"Never mind the money. You will have plenty of that," said the father.

It was duly arranged that the wedding should take place at the end of the next trip, and on the strength of that there was much rejoicing at the villa, in which James Leigh heartily joined. He was pressed to stay all night with the happy family, but he said that he could not do so, owing to pressing official duties; so he bade his usual *adieux*, and slipped out into the balmy night and made his way aboard the vessel. He packed his belongings in a bag, woke the captain, who was asleep in his berth, shook hands with him, and said—

"Good-bye, Dutchy. *You* can do what you blessed well like, but I am off."

And before the captain had recovered from his sleepy amazement his mate had slipped over the side into a boat. That was the last Dutchy ever saw of his prospective brother-in-law.

James Leigh stowed himself away aboard a Yankee full-rigged packet-ship which had to sail the following morning, and when the coast was clear he made his appearance. He was subjected for a time to that brutal treatment which at one time disgraced the American mercantile marine,[3] but being a smart young fellow who could do the work of a competent seaman, and handle his "dukes" with aptitude, the officers began to show partiality towards him, and before many days he became quite a favourite with them and with the captain. To his surprise, when the vessel had been at Philadelphia a few days, he was asked to qualify for the second officer's berth. He received the compliment with modest reserve, but his inward

she asked them to be seated, her voice and accent gave the impression of a lady. She chatted quite freely to the sailors about their profession and the countries they had visited, which led them to suppose that the lady was a great traveller. She, however, told them that her knowledge was derived from books. Shortlegs was mute. While the others talked he was closely scrutinizing the surroundings. Their host was a tall, well-set man, with shifty, evil-looking eyes that were kept busy, as was his tongue. After they had been in the house some time, he asked them if they wished to stay all night.

"We don't want ter press yer, but if yer like we've got a comfortable room. But ye'll both 'ave to sleep in one bed."

"We don't mind that," said James Leigh. "Show us where it is."

They bade the lady good morning, as it was 2 a.m., and they were escorted upstairs to a moderately-furnished room with an iron bed, wooden washstand, wardrobe, two chairs, and canvased floor.

"Well, do you think it'll do?" asked the host.

"Yes," replied James, in a jaunty way. "We've slept in many a worse place than this, Shorty, haven't we? See that we're called at six in the morning, gov'nor."

"That's all right," said the shifty-eyed host; "we're early birds, we are, in this 'ere 'ouse. We goes to bed early too. Wot'll ye 'ave for breakfast?"

"Never mind breakfast; we'll get that when we get aboard," replied Leigh. "Good-night; it's very good of you to put us up."

The host remarked that he was pleased to do a kindness to anybody, but especially to sailors, and then he slid out of the room. Shortlegs watched him downstairs, then closed the door. When he looked round his second officer was half undressed. He whispered to him not to undress, and that if he knew as much about bugs as he did he would need no telling.

"Oh! d—— the bugs and everything else. I'm in for a good nap."

"Well," said Shortlegs, "you may do as you like, but I'm a-going to keep my clothes on."

Jim, however, did not heed his companion's advice; he undressed, jumped into bed, and was soon asleep. Shortlegs sat smoking his pipe for a while, then rose and commenced a survey of the room. He looked under the bed, into a cupboard, behind the curtains, and then sat down and pondered over their strange experience. At last he pulled his boots and coat off, and was preparing to get into bed, when it occurred to him that he had not examined the wardrobe; so he jumped up, opened the door, stood gazing at the inside, closed the door, went to the bed, shook his mate into consciousness, and speaking in a loud whisper, he said—

"Jim, for God's sake get up!"

"What for?" said Jim.

"Because there's a dead 'un in the wardrobe," replied Shortlegs.

"A what?" asked Mr. Leigh.

"A corpse," responded his companion.

"Go on, don't talk such rot!"

"Very well, look for yourself," said the boatswain, who again opened the door, and exposed the dead body to view. James Leigh turned pallid and almost inarticulate. He could only touch his friend on the shoulder, and utter—

"My God, where are we? What shall we do with the corpse?"

Visions of being had up for murder had seized him. But he was quickly pulled up by his more discreet shipmate, who told him to cease speaking, allow the dead 'un to remain where he was, keep their boots off, open the window quietly, see how far it was to drop or to lower themselves down with the bedclothes. This being done, they found the plan of escape impracticable without being "nabbed," so they took the bold resolve of going out as they had come in, with their boots on. Before they had got half-way down the stairs they heard suppressed conversation. It was evident they were detected.

"Use your knuckle-duster, Jim, if necessary, and charge them with murder," whispered Shortlegs.

"You leave that to me, Shorty; I'm going to get out of this."

When they reached the bottom of the stairs, the room door, which was ajar, opened, and the man who showed them upstairs stood before them. He was in his sleeping clothes. They requested him to open the outer door and let them out, as they did not desire to remain any longer in the house. He asked why they were leaving comfortable lodgings on such a night. Jim being the spokesman, said they didn't like sleeping with corpses, and raising his voice with nervous courage, declared that if the door was not immediately opened he would stand a good chance of being put in the wardrobe where the other poor devil was. The wretched bully, shivering with passion and sudden fear, made a grab at Jim, and in an instant he was lying on the floor, and the two sailors opened the door and stepped out into the cold fog.

"My God, what an experience!" said Shorty. "What a lucky thing I looked in the wardrobe. We might have been given up to the police as the murderers; and that lady, as we thought, what a demon she must be to be connected with such."

"My dear fellow," said the second mate, "don't say anything wrong against the lady. How do we know but she is a prisoner, or in some way beholden to the rascal. What a strange thing she never appeared. I wonder if she was there. She must have been, as we heard voices."

"That's right enough," said the boatswain; "but was it her voice?"

"I never thought of that, Shorty. What d'ye say if we go back and try and learn more about this mysterious affair?"

"Not me," said Shorty; "I've had enough of this kind of experience."

"But," remonstrated the officer, "suppose the lady is in captivity?"

"Never mind that, boss. I don't care if there were twenty blessed women in captivity. I'm not going back, because I thinks the lady is in the swim."

"Nonsense, Shorts. She is an educated woman!"

"Yes; and I've heard, boss, of educated women doin' funny things. How d'ye know but it's her husband that's in the wardrobe, gov'nor? No, no; I knows some of these 'ere ladies, and I'm not a-going to mix myself up with them. And if you takes my advice you'll stick to me and get aboard as soon as we can. And keep this 'ere affair mum, or we may have a visit from some of her Majesty's detectives."

"Well," ejaculated James Leigh, "it is a mystery, and must remain such so far as we are concerned. But I am tempted to tell the police, as I feel certain that woman cannot be there of her own free will."

"Woman be d— —d, boss! How do you know, as I said before, that she's not at the bottom of it? You never knew an affair like this that a woman had not her hand in it; and if you are going to give information, don't introduce your humble servant, who has his own ideas of this 'ere person."

The young fellows had talked on ever since they left the tomb of the dead, unheeding the direction in which they were going. When the fog cleared they found themselves amidst the East End slums, environed by all that was villainous. They were not long in winding their way aboard the *Betty Sharp*. The night's exploits made a deep impression on James Leigh; it caused him to review the Bohemian career he had lived ever since he ran away from the *Pacific* in Chili. He resolved to pay a visit to his home in Wales, as he was so near, and in spite of strong protestations on the part of the captain he resigned his post. There was great rejoicing in the little village when he unexpectedly made his appearance. The news of the mutiny aboard the *Pacific*, and the tragic end of the captain, officers, and part of the crew preceded him. His family had blamed him for leaving at Iquique. They now said he had been guided by a strange but merciful Providence to his old home. He told the eager listeners of the family circle many tales of daring adventure as they sat in the cosy room by the fire, but whenever the gruesome figure of the dead man in the wardrobe crossed his mind he became reticent and pensive. These lapses did not go unnoticed, and he was often pressed for the cause of so sudden a change from mirth to sullen silence.

"I will tell you what it is," said he; "a corpse is the cause."

And then he told them all about it. James Leigh's change of life, manner, and habits dated from the dreaded night when he saw with his own eyes the ghastly figure of what he believed to be a murdered man. From being a roving, reckless, devil-may-care sailor, he settled into a steady, ambitious, capable man. He married a Welsh girl after his own heart, and forgot all about the daughter of the old Spaniard, who, if subsequent accounts were correct, pined for his return to Chili. Mrs. Leigh resented any allusion to the Spanish maiden. She always reminded her husband that people should marry their own countrywomen, and that instead of thinking of her he should be using his mind in attaining that knowledge that would enable him to reach the height of his profession. He was not long in satisfying the lady's ambition and his own. In less than five years from leaving the Yankee ship he was in command of a smart, up-to-date English steamer, trading between Mozambique and Zanzibar, trafficking in slaves and other merchandise. He made heaps of money for his owners, and was gifted with an aptitude for never neglecting himself in matters of finance. In due course the trade collapsed, and he was ordered to bring his vessel home. By this time his savings from several sources had accumulated to a decent little fortune, and with it he resolved to start business on his own account. He sought the aid of a few friends, and was enabled to purchase a small steamer. It was while he was on a visit to this much-boasted-of craft that he came across Shorty at a fair outside Cardiff. The rugged ex-boatswain had a machine for trying strength, and asked him to have a go. Captain Leigh recognized his old shipmate by a defect in his speech, and made himself known. Shorty was filled with delight, and would have given him the whole show. He rushed off, called out to a lady who was attending to the machine, and brought her to be introduced.

"This is my bit o' cracklen, Jim. She's a good 'un, she is. Now, don't ye be a-fallin' in love with her, James, as you used to with the other girls out in Chili, ancetera, ancetera. Don't ye reckonize her? Don't ye remember that fine hotel we landed in, and the wardrobe and one or two other incidents?"

"I do," said Captain James Leigh; "but surely this is not?"

"Yes, it is," said the proud husband. "It's she, isn't it, chubby?"

The lady merely nodded her head and smiled.

"Then what have you been doing, Shorty, all these years?"

"This," said he, pointing to the show. "I never got over the 'orror of that night, so I made my mind up not to go a rovin' agen; and this 'ere girl, that I thought so badly of, 'as helped me to make a livin' ever since I came across her. Very queer, you was right; she was sort o' confined to the 'ouse, but had nothin' to do with the corpse. She didn't know of it until I told her."

"My God! don't talk of it, Shorts. I cannot bear to think of it even now. But how did you pick her up?"

"At the docks," said John Shorts. "She came to look for us, and I took on with her and got married."

"You must have had a strong belief in her."

"Yes; and so would you if you knew her as I do. I'd trust my money, and my life, and everything with her. D'ye see that waggon of mats and baskets? That's her department; started on her own 'ook. My word, she's a daisy."

"Well, Shorty, I'm delighted to see you. And now I must be going. You seem quite happy."

"Happy," said the boatswain, "that's not a name for it. It's 'eaven on earth this 'ere thing," looking and pointing at his wife. Breaking off quickly, he said, "'Ave ye ever heard from Chili, Jim?"

"Oh yes," said he; "I had a letter only the other day from Dutchy. The old owner died, and left all his money to his two daughters and Dutchy, who married the eldest."

"That's a bit thick, isn't it, Jim—for that fat Dutchman to go wandering about the Spanish Main doin' all sorts of things, and then fall on his feet like this?"

"Well," said Jim, "you have fallen on your feet, so you say; and I'm sure I have."

"That's right," said Shorts. "I wasn't thinken' that the wife was standin' by."

The lady quietly smiled, shook hands with her husband's late chum, and walked off towards her caravan. Captain Leigh endeavoured to draw Shorty to tell him about his wife, but the old sailor evaded all his questions.

"Well," said Leigh, "this has been a joyful meeting to me, and if we never met again, God bless you!"

"The same to you, Jim," said Shorts. "Good-bye, old chap."

The two men never did meet again. James Leigh is now a prosperous merchant, and may be seen any day in a smart-cut "frocker" and silk hat, having his lunch at a bar, surrounded with kindred spirits, telling his wonderful tales—some truthful, others well padded, but all interesting.

FOOTNOTES

[3] It may be said in passing that America at that period, and for some years later, supplied Great Britain and other nations with the finest and fastest ships afloat, large and small. The Americans have always had a reputation of doing things on a large scale. Unmistakably their vessels were bad to beat. Their crews were well paid and well fed. They had the best cooks and stewards in the world; but the inadequacy of their manning, and the cruel treatment of the poor wretches who composed the crew, was a national disgrace. An American vessel with a mediocre crew aboard was nothing short of a hell afloat, and even with an average lot of men it was little better, unless they had the courage and the capacity to straighten the officers out, which was sometimes done with salutary effect.